THE AMERICAN ITALIANS

D0838722

MINORITIES IN AMERICAN LIFE SERIES

General Editor: Alexander DeConde
University of California, Santa Barbara

THE IRISH IN THE UNITED STATES, John B. Duff, Seton Hall University

THE CHALLENGE OF THE AMERICAN DREAM: THE CHINESE IN THE UNITED STATES, Francis L. K. Hsu, Northwestern University

THE AMERICAN ITALIANS: THEIR HISTORY AND CULTURE, Andrew F. Rolle, Occidental College

FORTHCOMING

JEWISH CULTURE IN THE UNITED STATES IN THE 20TH CENTURY, Milton Plesur, State University of New York at Buffalo

THE NEGRO CULTURE IN THE SOUTH SINCE THE CIVIL WAR, Arnold H. Taylor, University of Connecticut

THE AMERICAN ITALIANS:

Their History and Culture

Andrew F. Rolle

Cleland Professor of History

Occidental College

Wadsworth Publishing Company, Inc., Belmont, California

ISBN–0–534–00235–8
L. C. Cat. Card No. 72–84067

Printed in the United States of America

1 2 3 4 5 6 7 8 9 10—76 75 74 73 72

OTHER BOOKS BY ANDREW ROLLE

Riviera Path (Mondadori, Milan, 1948)

An American in California (Huntington Library, San Marino, 1956)

The Road to Virginia City (University of Oklahoma Press, 1960)

Lincoln, a Contemporary Portrait, with Allan Nevins, Irving Stone, and others (Doubleday, New York, 1962)

Occidental College—The First Seventy-Five Years (Ward Ritchie Press, Los Angeles, 1962)

California: A History (T. Y. Crowell, New York, 1963, 2d ed., 1969)

A Century of Dishonor: The Early Crusade for Indian Reform (Harper's, New York, 1965), Editor, Helen Hunt Jackson.

The Lost Cause: Confederate Exiles in Mexico (University of Oklahoma Press, 1965), Preface by A. L. Rowse.

California: A Students' Guide to Localized History (Columbia University Press, New York, 1966)

The Golden State (T. Y. Crowell, New York, 1965)

Los Angeles: A Students' Guide to Localized History (Columbia University Press, New York, 1966)

The Immigrant Upraised: Italian Adventurers and Colonists in an Expanding America (University of Oklahoma Press, 1968) Preface by Ray Allen Billington. Reprinted as *Emigranti Vittoriosi* by Mondadori, Milan with a new preface by Luigi Barzini.

Life in California (Peregrine Press, Salt Lake City, 1971), Editor, Alfred Robinson.

SERIES FOREWORD

The *Minorities in American Life* series is designed to illuminate hitherto-neglected areas of America's cultural diversity. Each author treats problems, areas, groups, or issues that cannot ordinarily be examined in depth in the usual surveys of American history and related subjects. Although all the volumes are connected to each other through the unifying theme of minority cultures, the series is flexible and open to a number of uses. For example, two or more volumes can be used as units in a comparative study. Each will bring out the distinctive features of an ethnic group, but together the books may show the common as well as the unique features and experiences of each minority studied.

In varying degrees every book includes narrative, analysis, and interpretation. Each is written simply, clearly, and intelligently by an authority on its subject, and all reflect the most recent scholarship. Some restate, with fresh insights, what scholars may already know; others present new syntheses, little-known data, or original ideas related to old concepts; and all are intended to stimulate thought, not merely to pass on information. By opening minority studies to young people, the series also meets a social and educational need. By providing short, sound, and readable books on their life and culture, and by accepting them on their own terms, the series accords minorities the justice and appreciation for their heritage that they have seldom received. By dealing with live issues in a historical context, it also makes the role of minority culture in American life meaningful to young people and opens new doors to an understanding of the American past and present.

Alexander DeConde

PREFACE

This book takes a historical approach to the immigrant experience as well as describing why immigrants left Italy, how they were changed by American culture, how they fared, and where they settled. After examining the immigrants' role within the political, economic, and cultural life of the United States, we discuss their current attitudes, problems of the second generation, and recent immigration. The term "Italian" in this volume concerns persons or concepts whose origins can be traced to the Italian peninsula from Sicily to Piedmont.

The best known and first Italian to land in the New World was, of course, Columbus. This volume does not, however, attempt to treat more than a few of the millions of individual Italians who migrated to America. Discussions of men like Mazzei and Vigo, important during the Revolutionary War, occur alongside considerations of explorers such as Tonty and Beltrami. The later major figures include La Guardia, Giannini, Fermi, Pastore, Volpe, and Alioto. Yet the book concerns more than the achievements of such individuals.

The mass migration occurring from the late nineteenth century onward needs fresh examination. Historians have become more sophisticated about what actually happened to immigrants after they landed. They were required—in subtle, albeit unconscious ways—to give up past loyalties and identities; "Americanization" meant partially denying one's heritage. This may have been painful for the educated, but the great mass of immigrants came from peasant villages with a past they were willing to forget. For such persons, America meant liberation rather than rigidity. As compared to the control of provincial landlords, even the bigoted cities of America provided mobility and opportunity rather than closed privilege. Furthermore, by the late nineteenth century, the European regions from which most immigrants came were becoming urban centers and national states. These larger communities were placing localism (*campanalismo*) under attack. European governments were poorly prepared to help displaced, unemployed peasants who flocked increasingly toward the cities for sustenance. Thus the appeal of distant America, and all its promises of opportunity that have become virtual clichés in our time.

Despite the discrimination and disguised bigotry that some immigrants encountered, few were too inflexible to change their old ways.

Difficulties arose not so much out of the European past as from the challenges of the new land. Elimination of distrust and suspicion ought, ideally, to have been easy in a pluralistic, relatively open, society. But sometimes the opposite occurred. There was new conflict between ethnic groups—over religion, jobs, housing, and social status. The blurring of ethnic lines alone seemed to accomplish assimilation —a term that has only recently become pejorative.

Many immigrants lived on in the urban centers of the eastern United States, both as contributors to and victims of rapid industrialization. As suggested in my previous book, *The Immigrant Upraised,* the Italian who went West experienced less alienation, accommodated quite rapidly to the new environment, and joined in the rural as well as urban growth of the country. Some of them, indeed, thereby lost their Italianate character and found a new identity. I continue to believe that the immigrant's ability to manipulate his environment has been underestimated.

In looking at the acculturative process, east or west, its negative by-products also emerge. In addition to discrimination, these include criminality and the unfathomable Mafia. A number of questions grow out of examining such subjects. Do persons of Italian background still experience discrimination? What is their current view of the old country? Who is immigrating today? What of the postwar vogue of imports from Italy (including fashions, furniture, autos, movies, and typewriters)?

Eventually, most immigrants and their children became anything but uprooted refugees. Casting off ancient folkways, they came to accept the middle-class American maxim that in the New World they were masters of their environment. Italians, like other nationalities, conformed to this ideal. Renouncing their distant villages, they viewed the United States as that place of hope they had heard about across the seas. If a family encountered bias, they would wear it down, just as its members had withstood the homeland's climatic, economic, and social inequities. Conformity to the American work ethic was sometimes unpleasant, indeed sordid; but settlers who knew their goals and who labored hard could create in this New World the environment they deserved. This was the creed of most immigrants. Transplanted, rather than uprooted, Italians were rewarded materially by a better day than they had known before, although admittedly not without suffering, privation, and prejudice.

In completing this volume I am grateful for the suggestions of Professor Alexander DeConde, editor of the series in which it appears, as well as of A. William Salomone, Wilson Professor of European History at The University of Rochester.

CONTENTS

The Mulberry Bend, c. 1888. Photograph by Jacob A. Riis. The Jacob A. Riis Collection, Museum of the City of New York.

Per Francesca

The Italian, especially the common Italian, is at once so complex and so simple that one can only smile at the strangers who think that in a year or so on the peninsula they have discovered the key to the Italian character. Paradox or not, it is easier to discover the complexity of Italians than their simplicity.

Carlo Sforza
The Real Italians

Chapter One

New World and Old

Before 1900, the majority of North America's immigrants had come from northern and western Europe. Our earliest culture and institutions reflected English rather than Latin traditions. Among the first Mediterranean travelers who came to the United States were clerics, scientists, or noblemen in search of adventure. Around the turn of the century a "new immigration" yearned for freedom and wealth across the seas, and a variety of southern European nationalities swarmed into New York's gateway. The Italians made up a large part of that movement. Social, economic, and political conditions on the Italian peninsula best explain why hundreds of thousands of these people left for the New World.

Since medieval times, periodic famines had existed even in Italy's "breadbasket provinces." By the end of the nineteenth century severe local taxes had been levied upon land, and widespread unemployment caused a deadening discontent. Landholding was generally restricted to large owners. In over-populated provinces, the best soil belonged to the nobility; small tenants were lease-holders or agricultural workers who labored for little return. Landlords demanded high rents and a sizable proportion of crops, leaving little for peasants to live on in the winter months. Furthermore, social apathy prevented correction of inequalities. There were some local uprisings, as in 1898 at Milan, where mobs defied government troops, but these were suppressed. Government, thus, came to be widely regarded as an enemy. Most persons had no appreciation for the possibility of cooperative group progress. Increased population only added to the poverty of village and farm folk.

In the late nineteenth century Italy was undergoing her unification, but the average Italian did not feel involved in that process. Only since 1870 had there been a united country. A good many of the immigrants to North America came from remote villages where local dialects and loyalties had worked against national unity. Furthermore, at a time when the country's focus should have been upon internal improvements, Italian bureaucratic leaders fanned the notion of acquiring a shaky empire in North Africa and in the Mediterranean. Their imperial adventures proved economically unrewarding, for Italy's marginal colonies required supportive internal taxation.

The land distribution promised by Giuseppe Garibaldi—Italy's George Washington—never materialized. Peasants struggled on, as they had for centuries, with a parched and stubborn soil. Poor rainfall in addition to numerous high mountain barriers reduced tillable acreage on the spiny peninsula. Small villages clung to rocky hillsides, their surrounding topsoil drained away by centuries of erosion. After 1900, when Italy's population reached a density of more than 100 persons per square mile, remote yet sizable tracts of land located in swamps and inaccessible mountains remained uninhabitable. In the south, rain was either so scarce or so abundant as to cause unpredictable droughts or floods. Conversely, peasants living in marshes were at the mercy of ravaging cholera and malaria. In addition to earthquakes and depleted soil, Italy lacked basic mineral resources, especially coal and iron. Financial capital to develop industry and commerce was also lacking; interest rates on loans frequently stood at 50 percent per year.

Depressed by a psychology of scarcity, little wonder that whole villages became depopulated. During 1900 an estimated million laborers spent up to two months annually working away from their own provinces. Large numbers of Italians already had emigrated to South America, despite its political instability and health hazards. In Brazil, one yellow fever epidemic alone claimed 9000 Italian lives. Such factors increased the attraction of North America.

The myths that everyone could rise to the top, regardless of origin or religion, and that the United States would provide a refuge for the unfortunate and maltreated now seem trite. But immigrants acted upon such clichés. A belief in the American sense of fair play and equal opportunity unlocked the immigrant heart.

Earlier, an Italianate vogue among cultured Americans had led to other romantic notions about Italy's antiquity. By the end of the eighteenth century, Mediterranean styles of art and architecture had emerged in the eastern United States. But this sentimental craze for things Roman and Greek was indulged in only by relatively wealthy Americans, reflecting contacts with Italians who were educated and artistic. Most Americans knew little about Italians to prepare them for the immigrant avalanche about to descend upon them.

The majority of Italians enroute to America came from the countryside. Some peasants had not seen a major city before reaching coastal embarkation points. After 1880, the ports of Genoa, Naples, and Palermo became great human expatriation centers. To discourage crowds from milling about these ports, steamship companies were forbidden from advertising more than the bare details of sailing dates. Across the ocean, as many as 15,000 Italians reached Ellis Island in a single day. In 1880 steerage passenger rates from Naples to New York were only $15; they grew to $28 by 1900.

The federal census of 1900 recorded that, since 1820 (no immigration records were kept before that date) some 20 million newcomers had entered the United States and that one third of the nation consisted of foreign-born residents or their children. United States immigration reached a crest in 1907, when 1,285,000 foreigners arrived. In that year alone, more Italians departed their homeland than the entire population of Venice. In 1913, one person in 40 left Italy; the majority emigrated from southern Italy, often from Calabria, the Abruzzi district, or Sicily.

Italian-born persons would one day comprise the second largest foreign element in the United States. By 1910 there were already over two million native-born Italians in this country. In the following decade another 1,109,524 of them appeared. By 1972 approximately 11 percent of the total population of the United States were of Italian descent.

The majority of immigrants fortunately arrived when workers were sorely needed. Wages were two to five times higher in the United States than at home. In 1903, for example, Sicilian common laborers (*braccianti*) were paid the equivalent of only 25 cents for 12 hours of work. In the United States one could count on earning wages of $1.50 per day. Italians played an important role in constructing railroads, bridges, subways, and in carving out agricultural lands in the new continent.

What was it like to leave one's homeland for the new world? In 1910 Pascal d'Angelo, an immigrant who came to be called "the Pick and Shovel Poet," recorded why he had departed:

Our people have to emigrate. It is a matter of too much boundless life and too little space. . . . Every bit of cultivable soil is owned by those fortunate few who lord over us. Before spring comes over our valley all the obtainable land is rented out or given to the peasants for a season under usurious conditions, namely for three-fourths, one-half, or one-fourth of the crops. . . . But now there was escape from the rich landowners, from the terrors of drought, from the spectre of starvation, in the boundless Americas out of which people returned with fabulous tales and thousands of liras—riches unheard of before among peasants.[1]

No matter how rich they found the new land to be, a temporary sense of loneliness gripped d'Angelo and other immigrants. It is, therefore, no wonder that most of those who arrived on the eastern tidewater of the United States reconstructed replicas of their hometown villages along its crowded city blocks.

When an Italian spoke of his *paese* he did not mean Italy; he meant the particular part of Italy where he was born. Village rather than country was the unifying factor. D'Angelo put it this way: "We fellow townsmen in this strange land clung desperately to one another. To be separated from our relatives and friends and to work alone was something that frightened us, old and young. So we were ready to undergo a good deal of hardship before we would even consider breaking up the gang." This clinging to each other existed among other ethnic groups as well. A district composed of a particular nationality frequently sustained itself with little change from generation to generation.

Some Italians, however, looked westward. They yearned for soil to till and countryside to settle. Today it is difficult to imagine how lonely and uninformed immigrants were concerning conditions beyond the eastern seaboard. Few reliable sources of information were easily available to them. One of the best known guidebooks, Edward H. Hall's *Travelers', Miners', and Emigrants' Guide and Handbook,* published in London in 1867, instructed newly-debarked persons how they could go west from New York City. It is, however, safe to assume that most immigrants, even if they could read English, never saw the pages of such a guide. Even in the cities it was not easy to make one's way outside the ghettos that lined Mulberry Street in New York and Federal Hill in Providence.

To pass beyond the squalor of the cities toward the grandeur of the West's prairies and mountains was to separate oneself finally from

---

[1] Pasquale d'Angelo, *Pascal D'Angelo, Son of Italy* (New York, 1924), p. 55.

memories of Europe. To a degree, such thinking may have been escapist. But the call of virgin lands acted like a magnet for immigrants with farm backgrounds. Any move beyond the steel and concrete skyline of America's eastern cities remained complicated. Not only did further travel require money which the Italian did not have, but it meant crossing great distances of unfamiliar land. When d'Angelo decided to go inland only a few hundred miles, he recorded his anxiety. "We had about two hours to get ready. We all went to get our bundles and our one valise in which we had our common possessions. These consisted of pots, four old tin plates, rather yellow-looking, some spoons and forks for use in case we should ever dare to cook macaroni." It was a big move to travel toward a remote coal mine in Pennsylvania or Ohio. To reach a lumber camp in the Pacific Northwest seemed beyond wisdom. Yet every state in the nation gained by the migration of the foreign-born, whether as farmers, railroad workers, miners, or lumberjacks.

Traffic between Italy and the United States passed in both directions; some immigrants returned to the old country in disgust after being cheated by American or Italian contractors called *padroni*. Most, however, considered life in America permanent and sent for their families, who then took up the habits and language of the Anglo. Even while beginning a new life, the Italians provided a humanizing influence. They seemed to soften America's harsh contours. As one looks at the mosaics they put together in the New York subways or at the terrazzo and statuary art they fashioned, a genuine desire to go beyond the work ethic and to improve the chosen land is apparent.

Even though the Italians were Mediterranean, and linked to the French, Spanish, and Greeks in background, they remained apart from other nationalities. Although the Irish were usually Catholic, Italians grouped them together with the Scandinavians and Germans.

Today almost every American city has leaders whose fathers (or who themselves) started out as Italian immigrant laborers and became politicians, lawyers, medical men, musicians, or artists. Who has not heard of New York's Mayor Fiorello LaGuardia or, more recently, of Mayor Joseph Alioto in San Francisco? Banker A. P. Giannini, physicist Enrico Fermi, Senator John Pastore, and baseball's Joe Di Maggio are also familiar names.

Italian modes of living and eating have likewise become popular. Ethnic grocery stores and restaurants by the thousands have sprung up in American metropolitan communities as well as in out-of-the-way places where Italians settled, although the new society did water down traditional ways of life somewhat. American soldiers who served in two world wars spent time in Italy, returning to the United States with a new appreciation for its life style. After World War II tourists flocked to Italy to visit the Vatican and admire the paintings of Leonardo da Vinci, as well as the statues of Michelangelo, and to sit in the *trattorias* of Rome. In an age when Pope John XXIII became a congenial international favorite, the Eternal City and its fountains beckoned anew.

But we are getting ahead of our story. Let us now turn to how the Italian experience in North America actually began.

Chapter One Bibliography

In contrast to a few years ago, a growing literature continues to emerge about all ethnic groups. This material runs from the self–congratulatory fileo-pietism of earlier days to a latter-day despair. Some second–generation ethnic historians seem determined to maintain the myth that upward mobility has not occurred. Forming part of a general rebellion against the American success ethic, they do not wish to bask in the sunshine of achievements won by their parents and grandparents. Rather, they choose to look at the more somber side of the immigration record, tending to feature prejudice and unfairness toward foreigners rather than material attainments wrested against great odds.

Useful books on the general immigration theme are: Louis Adamic, *A Nation of Nations* (New York, 1945); Theodore C. Blegen, ed., *Land of Their Choice: The Immigrants Write Home* (Minneapolis, 1955); Marcus Lee Hanson, *The Immigrant in American History* (Cambridge, 1940); John Higham, *Strangers in the Land* (New Brunswick, 1955); Irene D. Jaworski, *Becoming American: The Problems of Immigrants and Their Children* (New York, 1960); Maldwyn A. Jones, *American Immigration* (Chicago, 1960); John F. Kennedy, *A Nation of Immigrants*, rev. ed. (New York, 1964); R. A. Schermerhorn, *These Our People: Minorities in American Culture* (Boston, 1949); William Carlson, *Americans in the Making: The Natural History of the Assimilation of Immigrants* (New York, 1939); Carl Wittke, *We Who Built America: The Saga of the Immigrant*, rev. ed. (Cleveland, 1964); and Philip Taylor, *The Distant Magnet* (New York, 1971).

Renewed interest in immigration and its effects in America has resulted in several recent studies. Useful books are: John J. Appel, ed., *The New Immigration* (New York, 1970); Andrew Greeley, *Why Can't They Be Like Us?* (New York, 1969); and Judith Kramer, *The American Minority Community* (New York, 1970).

Volumes specifically about Italians include: Luigi Barzini, *The Italians* (New York, 1964), which does not concern immigration but helps readers to understand the Italian character; Pascal d'Angelo's *Pascal D'Angelo, Son of Italy* (New York, 1924) is an autobiography which poignantly reveals the feelings of a newcomer to America; The Federal Writer's Project volume, *The Italian of New York* (New York, 1938), written before World War II, is still an excellent source.

Some of the most valuable books on the Italian immigrant are old or out of print. Eliot Lord, et al., *The Italian in America* (New York, 1905), is such an early study; Robert F. Foerster, *The Italian Emigration of Our Times* (Cambridge, 1919), is only partly devoted to United States immigration and to its Italian background; Emilio Goggio, *Italians in American History* (New York, 1930), is a pamphlet; Luciano Iorizzo and Salvatore Mondello, *The Italian Americans* (New York, 1971), is a recent interpretation; Michael A. Musmanno, *The Story of the Italians in America* (New York, 1965), is a glorified account of success in this country; Lawrence Pisani, *The Italian in America, a Social Study and History* (New York, 1957), is a sociological interpretation. Along similar lines is Joseph Lopreato, *Italian Americans* (New York, 1970). Andrew F. Rolle, *The Immigrant Upraised: Italian Adventurers and Colonists in an Expanding America* (Norman, Oklahoma, 1968) interprets the assimilation of the Italian immigrant, particularly in the American West. For those who read Italian, another version has been published in Italy entitled *Gli Emigrati Vittoriosi* (Milan, 1972).

Giovanni Schiavo's two volumes, *Four Centuries of Italian American History* (New York, 1952) and his *Italians in America before the Civil War* (New York, 1934) are useful for enumerating the contributions of specific Italians although these books do not discuss social or adjustment problems. Silvano Tomasi and Madeline H. Engel, eds., *The Italian Experience in the United States* (New York, 1970), is an attempt to understand the American Italians in light of modern ethnic studies. Its ten articles by various authors discuss the impact of Italian and American society on individuals, institutions, and the return migration. Rudolf Glanz, *Italian and Jew* (New York, 1970), is a comparison of Jewish and Italian immigrants in their quest for acculturation. Giuseppe Prezzolini, *I Trapiantati* (Milan, 1965) remains untranslated. This excellent work is virtually unknown in this country.

Two bibliographies that list books about Italian–Americans are: Francesco Cordasco and Salvatore La Gumina, *Italians in the United States: A Bibliography of Reports, Texts, Critical Studies, and Related Materials* (New York, 1972); Joseph Velikonja, *Italians in the United States* (Carbondale, Illinois, 1963).

Chapter Two

The Exploring Italians

America could have been called Columbia after Christopher Columbus, the imaginative Genoese who convinced the Spanish court to support his pathfinding voyage. Even though the North American coastline might have been touched before by others, Columbus is considered the discoverer. His voyage to America was no accident. Columbus was a knowledgeable seaman who studied long and planned carefully for his adventure. He did not know, however, that he was stepping onto a new continent after his tiny *Santa Maria* landed on the coast of San Salvador; he assumed he had reached an eastern shore of Asia.

On three succeeding trips to the New World, Columbus brought with him carpenters, seeds, and implements to succor Spain's new settlements. Even though he gained no personal reward from his discovery, his dying request was to be buried in the land he had found. Accordingly, his body was transported to Santo Domingo, one of the islands discovered on his first trip. Columbus's tomb is in the Cathedral of Santo Domingo, the oldest in America. No statue exists there to mark the momentous discovery, but monuments, streets, towns, and universities in the United States are named after him. As early as 1849, the city of Boston erected a statue in his honor. Songs and annual Columbus Day festivities throughout the Americas celebrate his voyage.

Before the 1860s Italy was a series of city-states. Furthermore, there was no "New Italy" in the Americas as there had come to be a "New Spain" or a "New France." Yet the empires of Spain, England, France, and Portugal depended heavily on Italian navigators and seamen who served under their foreign flags. One third of Magellan's fleet was made up of Italian sailors. The story of these early mariners is fragmented and buried in the records of other countries.

In 1497 John Cabot (actually Giovanni Caboto of Venice) sailed English ships along the coast of North America. His discoveries gave England legal claim to that part of the continent and opened the way for her settlers. Later his son, Sebastian Cabot, made further voyages in the service of both Spain and England. He repeatedly attempted to discover a northwestern route to the East, which increased knowledge of the New World.

Amerigo Vespucci, a later Florentine explorer, vividly described the distant lands discovered by Columbus. Cartographers thereafter came to use the name "America" on maps of the Western Hemisphere. Vespucci sailed along the coast of South America and was probably the first European to sight what the Spaniards later called Cape Canaveral, now Cape Kennedy.

In 1523 Giovanni da Verrazzano was the first European to reach New York Bay. He too drew a map and described the area from Canada to South Carolina. Because he sailed under a French flag, France based its claim to land in the New World from the date of that voyage. Another result of Verrazzano's discoveries was the confirmation that this new area was not a part of Asia, but an entity in itself.

An explorational scramble that developed by the 1540s saw the Spanish explorer Hernando de Soto opening up the Mississippi delta area for settlement. Italians were in his party. Individually and in groups, priests, soldiers, and adventurers followed explorers into the Spanish southwestern portion of what would become the United States long before the Pilgrims settled on the east coast.

In that vanguard was Fray Marcos de Niza—or Fra Marco da Nizza (1495–1558)—a Franciscan priest in the service of Spain. This cleric's exciting if inaccurate observations about present-day Arizona and New Mexico led to Coronado's famous expedition of 1540 which penetrated the mainland northward from Mexico City. By 1539, Fray Marcos had spent eight years wandering, trail-breaking, and establishing Spanish missions in the future American Southwest. He incorrectly described Indian whitewashed adobe huts that glimmered in the desert sun as having golden walls, which fortified an earlier legend about a "golden city—"El Dorado." Although the Spaniards did not subsequently find other "golden cities," explorers soon traversed a previously unknown territory. Coronado, for example, penetrated the mainland as far as present-day Kansas. Fray Marcos had unwittingly misled his superiors about the wealth of this area.

Fray Marcos was to be followed to the arid, windswept southwestern provinces by an Italian of more diverse talents. Eusebio Francesco Kino was the most prominent of various Italian Jesuits sent there. In 1678 Kino left Genoa for Spain, not reaching Mexico until three years later. His activities were many. The cattle industry of our Southwest dates in large measure from the disparate ranchos established by him throughout a path 250 miles wide. At the missions he founded, Kino not only introduced several varieties of livestock, but European grains and such fruits as grapes and pomegranates. Kino has also been credited with making the first astronomical observations in western America. His cartographical studies implemented the Spanish advance northward from Mexico. In 1683 Kino was appointed royal cosmographer of an expedition which tried to colonize Baja California. Between 1698 and 1701 he prepared maps printed in Paris showing for the first time that California was not an island. He also made improvements in mapping Spain's North American empire from the Colorado River to the Gulf of Mexico.

Kino, on horseback or afoot, made some 50 journeys of 100 to 1000 miles in length. These included six trips to the Gila River, two to the land of the Yumas on the Colorado, and one into what was then vaguely called "California." Kino, who covered from 25 to 75 miles per day, was indeed the "padre on horseback" that his biographer, Herbert Eugene Bolton, once called him. Towns in the Southwest grew up around Kino's missions.

After 1687 Kino established some 20 missions in "Greater Sonora." In the area to become the United States, the most important of these was San Xavier del Bac, now a national monument near Tucson. Kino died in 1711 in the mission village of Santa Magdalena, which he had founded. In 1965 Kino's statue was unveiled in the United States Capitol at Washington, a symbol of the Jesuit "black robes" who contributed their learning and personal dedication to Spain's empire.

Until late in the eighteenth century, Spain claimed most of the Pacific region up to what is now the Canadian boundary. As early as 1541 Girolamo Benzoni, a Milanese, wandered throughout what is now greater Mexico. He wrote a history and description of the region entitled *History of the New World* (1565); reprinted in various languages, it acquainted Europeans with the geography of North America. Similarly effective in adding to Europe's knowledge of Mexico was the book *The Idea of a New General History of Middle America* (1746) by the Italian chronicler, Lorenzo Boturini-Beneduci.

Yet another Italian traveler, Dr. Giovanni Francesco Gemelli-Careri, undertook a round-the-world voyage from 1693 to 1697. The last part of his trip was aboard a Manila galleon, sailing between the Philippines and Acapulco, Mexico. The closest Careri came to what is today the continental United States was the island group that he called Saint Catherine's in his six-volume *Voyage around the World.* This was probably in the Santa Barbara Channel, off southern California. Careri left one of the best existing accounts of a voyage on a Manila galleon; it was published in 1699, the year after he returned to Italy, and aroused much interest concerning Spain's New World empire.

The first Italian to anchor on the California coast was Captain Alessandro Malaspina who, in the late eighteenth century, commanded an international exploratory expedition which lasted more than five years. Malaspina had entered the Spanish maritime service early in life and distinguished himself sufficiently by his middle thirties to head this important scientific venture. Malaspina sailed up the west coast of Mexico from Acapulco as far as Alaska. He vainly sought a reputedly more direct passageway to the Far East called the straits of Anian for which mariners had searched for decades. As Malaspina sailed along the coast of today's British Columbia, he noted the insularity of Nootka Island, sounded the Strait of Juan de Fuca, and named various landmarks. There exist today a Malaspina Glacier, a Malaspina Strait, and a Malaspina Peak. After making various explorations, he sailed back down the northwest coast to California. At Monterey on September 16, 1791, Malaspina put ashore a corpse (one John Green who had shipped as a gunner at Cadiz), probably the first American in California. A description of Malaspina in California appears in *The Circumnavigation of the World by the Corvettes "Descubierta" and "Atrevida" under the Command of Captain D. Alejandro Malaspina from 1789 to 1794,* printed in 1885, long after his death at Mulazzo, Lunigiana, in 1809.

While such Italians helped to secure Spain's claims upon its remote frontiers, others entered the service of yet another foreign power. By the seventeenth century the North American fur trade had placed France's vanguard of settlement hundreds of miles inland from her colonization bases on the Saint Lawrence River. By 1679 Robert Cavelier de La Salle had reached the Illinois country where he claimed the major waterways of the Mississippi basin for King Louis XIV.

Accompanying La Salle was the soldier of fortune Henry de Tonty (or Tonti). Born an Italian, he came from a family with a record of service to the King of France. A brother, Alfonso, also became a French army officer in America, operating as a captain with Cadillac at Detroit. For some years Alfonso was the civilian and military governor of that outpost, and a cousin commanded Fort Illinois. During a French expedition to Sicily, Henry de Tonty had lost his hand in combat and came to be feared among the Indians as "the man with the iron hand," a hooklike metal claw.

In the company of La Salle, Tonty reached the Illinois region in the winter of 1679–1680. At Lake Peoria they built Fort Crevecoeur. After La Salle headed back eastward, Tonty remained in command of the Illinois country. When La Salle rejoined Tonty he found that his subaltern had been wounded in a mutiny and that an Iroquois invasion had forced him northward in the dead of winter. In the Wisconsin woods, Tonty lived for weeks on roots and wild garlic buried beneath the snow. He finally reached safety at Green Bay.

For a quarter of a century Tonty, despite many hardships, was faithful to the flag he carried into the wilderness for France. Together with La Salle he returned to the Illinois country to build Fort Saint Louis. In April 1682, at the mouth of the Mississippi, La Salle and Tonty took possession of the great valley for the King of France in whose honor they named Louisiana. Tonty is also credited with building Fort Niagara as well as Tonty's Fort on the Arkansas River and with construction of the *Griffin*, probably the first vessel to cross the Great Lakes.

La Salle returned to France to recruit an expedition for a new colony on the Texas coast. In 1687, before Tonty could travel overland to meet La Salle, his old comrade-in-arms was murdered near the Brazos River. For 15 years thereafter, Tonty remained in command of much of the Mississippi region until his death in 1703. France was fortunate to have the loyalty of so superb an explorer. Had there been a unified Italy at the time, this forceful and vigorous man might not have worked for France. La Salle once wrote that his "energy and address make him equal to anything."

It is difficult to ascertain how many Italians served France before Britain acquired her North American empire. Several thousand Italians probably came to the New World under French auspices. As early as 1644, Italian soldiers and political exiles were in French Canadian military units raised by the Prince of Carignano. Various Piedmontese members of these military units settled in Louisiana. In 1720 John Law, the Scottish financier who became involved in a French colonization scandal known as the Mississippi Bubble, tried to recruit

Italians for his Mississippi Company. That year 250 of them shipped out of Genoa to New France. Among the Italians who gave their service to France or Spain, either for adventure or because of unsettled conditions in their homeland, some returned but many stayed on as settlers after their duties ended.

Chapter Two Bibliography

For information about Italian explorers, see the two Schiavo volumes, *Four Centuries of Italian–American History* and *Italians in America before the Civil War* as well as more modern works such as Pisani's *The Italian in America* and *The Italian–Americans* by Iorizzo and Mondello. A pamphlet by Emilio Goggio, entitled *Italians in American History* (New York, 1930), is also helpful.

The best volume on Kino is by Herbert Eugene Bolton, *Rim of Christendom* (New York, 1936). Others include Frank C. Lockwood, *With Padre Kino on the Trail* (Tucson, 1934) and Rufus Kay Wyllys, *Pioneer Padre, The Life and Times of Eusebio Kino* (Dallas, 1935). Ernest J. Burrus is the translator and editor of *Kino Reports to Headquarters* (Rome, 1954). See also Eugenia Ricci, *Il Padre Eusebio Chini, Esploratore Missionario della California e dell'Arizona* (Milan, 1930).

For works on Malaspina, see a recent book by Donald Cutter, ed., *Malaspina in California* (San Francisco, 1960), and E. Boni, *Malaspina* (Rome, 1935).

For information on Tonty, see John Carl Parish, *The Man with the Iron Hand* (Boston, 1913), and a section in Barbara Marinacci, *They Came From Italy: The Stories of Famous Italian–Americans* (New York, 1967). This book is for younger readers.

Chapter Three

Italians in the American Colonies

There were few Italians in the seventeenth-century English colonies, but court records, church registers, and tax lists do record some Italian names. In those years relatively few Europeans emigrated. A voyage across the Atlantic took several months and cost a great deal of money. Personal fortitude was also needed, for deaths enroute occurred from lack of water and food, shipwrecks, or attacks by pirates. The English colonies did, however, offer the inducements of land, money, and tax exemptions for needed craftsmen.

As early as 1622, Venetian glassmakers working in England came to Jamestown, Virginia, to pursue and teach their trade. By 1632, a few Italians had also settled in Maryland, the only place on the Atlantic seaboard north of Florida well populated by Catholics. Some Italians settled in Georgia and planted mulberry trees. Further north at New Amsterdam, a plantation was started in the 1630s by Peter Alberti.

The first sizable Italian migration to North America was a religious one, made up of Waldensians who came by way of Holland. The Dutch offered them free transportation to America, and on Christmas Day in 1656 over 100 left Holland. These Protestants were mostly from Piedmont, close to Italy's French and Swiss borders, and were persecuted in Catholic Italy. They settled in Delaware and New York.

More than 100 years later, in 1768, a second sizable immigration from Italy occurred. Andrew Turnbull organized a group headed for the English province of East Florida. Eight vessels carried 200 Greeks, 110 south Italians, and 1100 Minorcans. Their voyage lasted four months, with many deaths due to unhealthy shipboard conditions. After a semi-feudal system was imposed upon the settlers, and following an outbreak of malaria, a mutiny broke out. Carlo Forni led a group of 30 men to seize a boat with which to escape to Havana, Cuba, but a British armed vessel forced Forni's party back to the Florida Keys. He and his fellow escapees were hanged for piracy. Death by scurvy, gangrene, and malaria carried off others. By 1777 most of the remaining colonists had left for St. Augustine or the Bahamas. A few made it back to Europe.

In England's northern colonies, life for Italian settlers was better. By the time of the American Revolution, they were managing a few stores, operating hotels, or serving as carpenters, shoemakers, and general laborers. Some were doctors, lawyers, and of course musicians. Along the frontier beyond the coastal settlements, fur traders and trail breakers included Italians in their company.

During the revolution itself, one Italian became especially prominent. This was Philip Mazzei. Although Mazzei played no official role in the creation of the United States, he has been called an "assisting founding father." He was also a ghost writer for several revolutionary leaders. Before he came to America, this medical doctor and scholar had developed strong ideas about freedom, blaming the institution of monarchy for the lack of personal liberty in the eighteenth century. Mazzei had become restless in Italy so he moved to England. In London he met Benjamin Franklin who, with several friends, talked Mazzei into organizing a company to grow silkworms, olives, and wine grapes in Virginia. Accompanied by a small group of Italian *contadini,* Mazzei took seeds, plants, and farm tools along to America.

His venture proved successful. Impressed by Mazzei's industry, a nearby planter, Thomas Jefferson, placed a substantial acreage at his disposal for agricultural experimentation. Mazzei also met George Washington, James Madison, Patrick Henry, and other key colonial leaders. Eventually he found himself more involved with revolutionary ideas than with silkworms, olives, and grapes.

In fact, during the years preceding 1775, Mazzei's ideas were more radical than those held by most colonists. These men still had no intention of breaking their ties with England, but Mazzei felt no loyalty to the English system. His strong yearning for religious freedom grew out of harsh personal experiences in Europe, and he believed that America could not be a democracy while under British domination. An excellent speaker, he voiced these ideas to colonial audiences in English, stressing how to resist authority. Jefferson, especially, listened closely and later translated a series of articles by Mazzei under the pseudonym Furioso. As John F. Kennedy points out in his book *A Nation of Immigrants*, the very doctrine that " 'All Men Are Created Equal,' incorporated in the Declaration by Thomas Jefferson, was paraphrased from the writings of Philip Mazzei." Thomas Paine's pamphlet, *Common Sense* (1776), also included ideas originated by Mazzei.

When the Revolution began, Mazzei volunteered his services, but Patrick Henry insisted that he could help the colonials more effectively by using his pen and voice. Mazzei was asked (as an agent of Virginia) to seek funds for the revolutionary cause from influential friends in Europe. Although Mazzei helped to persuade the French to aid the struggling colonies, he unfortunately became involved in a controversy between the Virginia colony and the newly formed Continental government. Mazzei, coming from a Catholic culture, felt he was never quite trusted by many American colonists.

In 1784 Mazzei returned permanently to Europe. He wrote a book about the United States and corresponded regularly with his American friends, particularly Jefferson. When he died in 1816, Jefferson recalled: "His esteem in this country was very general; his early and zealous cooperation in the establishment of our independence having acquired for him here a great degree of favor."

During the time Mazzei inspired the colonials against England, another leader of Italian descent, William Paca, was active in Maryland's contribution to the fight for independence. Paca's forebears (who originally spelled their name Pacci) had emigrated first to England, then to America. In 1651 Maryland granted the family a tract of land, and they became wealthy planters by the end of the seventeenth century. Later Paca served in the Maryland legislature as well as in the Continental Congress. Also a prominent jurist, he was among those who renounced allegiance to the British crown, signing his name to the Declaration of Independence. In 1782 Paca became the third governor of Maryland.

Standard immigration histories mainly discuss the role of the Irish, Scots, or Germans in the Revolutionary War. It is difficult to know how many Italians took part in that struggle. Although relatively few of them served in the Continental Army, persons with Italian names—for example, Captains Richard Talliaferro and Ferdinando Finizzi—fought for the American cause. Some Italians were also Tories. A Colonel Lewis Nicola, indeed, proposed George Washington as King.

The revolutionary struggle also involved capturing a vast western territory; if that area had remained in the hands of England or France, the new nation could not have later claimed it. Beyond the Mississippi, Francesco Vigo (baptized Giuseppe Maria Francesco Vigo) ultimately became aide-de-camp to the American Commander in the West, George Rogers Clark, during the Revolution.

Vigo's career reads like a fictional adventure story. He was born at Mondovi, Piedmont, in 1747. At an early age he ran away from home and enlisted in the Spanish army. After a tour of duty in Cuba he was transferred to New Orleans. By 1772 he was in Saint Louis, still under Spanish control. Vigo later entered the fur trade after being discharged from military service. A skillful Indian trader, he bartered goods with other Europeans pouring into the Mississippi Valley. There he met an increasing number of American colonials, including Colonel Clark. Though only 26 years old, Clark was to become commander of American forces in the West in the Revolution.

Toward the end of 1778, when British and American forces came to blows in the old Northwest, Vigo decided to join Clark in a campaign against the British. Clark gathered 175 tough frontiersmen at Fort Pitt. They descended the Ohio River to Fort Massac. Clark and Vigo crossed Illinois, and in July 1778, wrested Kaskaskia and other fortifications, including Cahokia and Vincennes, from the British. Vigo exercised great influence over Clark's volunteers and played a unique part in the final fall of Fort Vincennes. First he allowed himself to be captured by a group of Indians friendly to the British and to be turned over by them to General Henry Hamilton, commander of the Vincennes garrison. Technically a prisoner, Vigo was allowed the run of the fort and he carefully observed its defenses. General Hamilton foolishly released Vigo on the promise that he would retire to Saint Louis. Instead, Vigo journeyed northward toward the American forces in the Mississippi Valley.

On February 2, 1779, Vigo reached Kaskaskia, where Clark had quartered his force. He convinced Clark that no time should be lost in attacking Fort Vincennes, then held by only a few British troops. Vigo not only gave Clark this valuable intelligence; he advanced Clark personal funds to undertake his march back across southern Illinois. Vigo also raised money from local traders—principally Frenchmen—who had turned against the British.

During Clark's march through torrential rains, Vigo helped him further. Because of his fur-trading forays, he was more than familiar with the area about to be attacked. At times their expedition waded for hours through water that reached their waists. Holding precious powder horns and firearms high above them, the men pushed on toward Vincennes. On February 23, 1779, they overwhelmed General Hamilton's startled British forces. Vigo remained with Clark during the rest of the Revolution.

Although Vigo shares with Clark responsibility for the campaign that ended British influence in the Northwest, both men fell into obscurity after their victory. Although Vigo visited President Washington in 1789 and briefly became a negotiator with the Indians for the new United States government, he was not reimbursed for his financing of Clark's critical last expedition. Yet he did become a member of the State Assembly at Vincennes. The county of Vigo was created in his name. He died there a pauper in 1836; his undertaker was unable to collect the $20 necessary to bury Vigo. Forty years later the United States government finally repaid his heirs $50,000 for their ancestor's role in helping to win the American Revolution in the West. Only in 1941, however, did President Franklin Roosevelt belatedly recognize Vigo's contribution by issuing a declaration: "To Colonel Francesco Vigo, a patriot of Italian birth, the United States are indebted, next to Clark, for the liberation of the Northwest regions."

Limited immigration from Italy and other countries continued during America's first years. The Revolution had given meaning to the theory that America was a refuge for oppressed persons. About this, President Washington once wrote: "The bosom of America is open to receive not only the Opulent and respectable Stranger, but the oppressed and persecuted of all Nations and Religions. . . ." There were some, however, who had doubts about encouraging mass immigration. Among these was President Jefferson. Though he wanted all to share in liberty, he was fearful that too many foreigners would somehow corrupt America, endangering its fragile democracy.

As early as the federal period, tough anti-foreign measures, including the Alien and Sedition Acts, were passed by the United States Congress. By 1815, the United States seems to have developed an immigration policy that reconciled its early misgivings: all who wanted to come were welcome, although no special privileges or inducements were to be made. The beginnings of later prejudice may have been born in that earlier attitude, unwittingly launched by Jefferson, one of Philip Mazzei's lifelong friends and a president who had taken great joy in his Italian travels.

Chapter Three Bibliography

The role of Italians in the American colonies is covered generally in Schiavo's two volumes, *Four Centuries of Italian–American History* and *Italians in America before the Civil War*, Pisani's *The Italian in America* and Iorizzo and Mondello's *The Italian–Americans*, as well as by Marinacci's *They Came from Italy*. Also useful are J. H. Mariano, *The Italian Contribution to American Democracy* (Boston, 1921) and Richard C. Garlick, *Italy and the Italians in Washington's Time* (New York, 1933). For information about Mazzei, consult Garlick's *Philip Mazzei, Friend of Jefferson* (New York, 1942). Howard Marraro has also written on Mazzei's generation in "Italo–Americans in Pennsylvania in the Eighteenth Century," *Pennsylvania History*, 7 (July 1940), 159–166. Books useful for studying Vigo are Goggio's *Italians in American History* and Bruno Roselli's *Vigo: A Forgotten Builder of the American Republic* (Boston, 1933).

Chapter Four

The Italians and an Emerging Culture

By the end of the eighteenth century, Americans who once focused upon taming the wilderness had turned toward cultural pursuits. Former colonials looked to ancient Italy for inspiration. Among them were the new American leaders Jefferson, Washington, and Franklin. Italians with whom they were in contact included teachers, architects, artists, musicians, and scientists. Italy's influence became especially strong in classical architecture, which can still be seen in public buildings as well as in private homes on the East Coast. Jefferson's Monticello was in the Mediterranean style.

Italian sculptors were also sought to decorate buildings and parks in the nation's capital. The first sculptor of note, Giuseppe Ceracchi, arrived there in 1791. He wished to design a monument to Liberty 100 feet high, including statues of the new country's founding fathers. Although Congress did not sanction the project, various patriots posed for Ceracchi and their busts still exist. The sculptor was later executed in France for plotting against Napoleon.

Philip Mazzei was asked to engage another noted sculptor, Antonio Canova, to design a figure of Liberty for the "Chamber of Representatives." Instead, he obtained the services of two young sculptors, Joseph Franzoni and John Andrei, who kept various craftsmen busy building monuments and statues in Washington. Antonio Meucci's plans for the Capitol building's dome followed the lines of St. Peter's in Rome, designed by Michelangelo. During 1814 some of his work and that of other Italian craftsmen was destroyed in the flames that consumed the Capitol. More artists came from Italy to replace these lost objets d'art.

The artist whose work is best known was Constantino Brumidi, who has been called "the Michelangelo of the United States Capitol." Before coming to America in 1852, Brumidi worked on frescoes at the Vatican. American artists resented the government hiring foreigners to decorate the new Capitol. In spite of this opposition, 72-year-old Brumidi began his massive frescoes on the circular ceiling of the Capitol dome, 180 feet above the floor, covering an area of 4664 square feet. Brumidi portrayed a veritable panorama of American history, with figures two to three times their natural size. He was supported by a suspended cage which was moved with ropes at his direction as he lay working on his back. At one point the supports slipped, and he fell. Seizing the rung of a ladder, the old man clung there until workmen came to the rescue. This shock, plus exhaustion, probably caused his death five months later. Only in 1950 was Brumidi's grave located; Congress then passed a bill to place a marker on it.

Filippo Costaggini continued work on Brumidi's immense fresco. At Costaggini's death a 30-foot area remained unpainted. The American artist Allyn Cox put the finishing touches on Brumidi's ambitious frescoes. Aside from his dome decoration, other Brumidi paintings line the corridors of the Capitol. The House of Representatives dining room has a large fresco of Washington at Yorktown signed "C. Brumidi, Artist, Citizen of the U.S."

Italian musicians were also present in American cities early in the country's history. In 1757 John Palma gave a concert in Philadelphia. A subscription concert was held 17 years later for a Signora Mazzanti, probably the first Italian opera diva in America; tickets sold for a dollar, and dancing followed. Nicholas Biferi, a harpsichordist, gave concerts in 1775 and started a school of music and dancing in New York, the first of its kind in North America. Later, from 1836 to 1872, Lorenzo Papanti became master of a well-known dancing academy in Boston.

President Jefferson recruited Italian bandsmen for a national military band. In 1805, fourteen of these formed the nucleus of what became the United States Marine Corps Band, changing it from fife and drum to a distinctive musical ensemble. Many of its directors have been Italian. (The father of New York Mayor Fiorello La Guardia was, incidentally, an army bandmaster). A friend of presidents Madison and Monroe was Filippo Traetta, a composer and music teacher in Boston, New York, and Philadelphia. The son of a Venetian musician, Traetta organized an "American Conservatorio" in Philadelphia. His "The Venetian Maskers" was the first opera written in North America. The first formal symphonic concert was given there by Giovanni Gualdo, also a composer.

Italian achievements in other arts, including drama, have long been recognized. A variety of early actors and actresses performed in their native tongue. Professional entertainers—ballet dancers, magicians, and jugglers—came to the United States either individually or in organized troupes. As early as 1805 there was an Italian Theater in New York, and in the 1830s Cleveland had a three-story Italian Hall with a theater on its top floor.

Lorenzo Da Ponte also popularized opera in this country. A man of many talents, the Maestro had been Mozart's librettist. Da Ponte spared no effort to bring Italian language, culture, books, and music to his adopted country. Through his efforts, North America's first opera house—styled in the European manner with boxes, silk curtains, and grand scenery—was built in New York.

Ferdinando Palmo established yet another opera house in New York. It opened in 1844 with a performance of Bellini's *I Puritani* and continued in operation until 1847. Meanwhile opera companies sprang up on the east coast, and scores of Italian singers toured the young country. Some stayed on permanently, both as performers and teachers.

From an early date New Orleans welcomed Italian musicians and artists. After the 1820s, musical events including the opera were regularly sponsored there. In 1836 alone, Bellini's *Norma* received ten performances in New Orleans. The great soprano Adelina Patti made her debut there in 1855. Her voice made her for many seasons the toast of the American operatic scene. She and her contralto sister, Amelia, sang with the Ghioni and Susini Italian Opera Company, as well as with the Italian Company of the Grand Theatre of Mexico.

In the nineteenth century, Italian opera penetrated into the American West, where female singers were treated like queens. They rode special railroad cars equipped with pianos, private dining rooms, and salons. An Italian traveler, Carlo Gardini, met an opera troupe that had covered 13,000 miles in three months, giving 85 standing-ovation performances. At Cheyenne he attended a version of Donizetti's *Lucia di Lammermoor*, which featured a chorus of more than 60 Italian singers from London's Covent Garden Company. The conductor was a Maestro Arditi, composer of the popular "Il Bacio," or "The Kiss." Gardini wrote, "the touching melodies of Donizetti heard in a still wild region where only a few years before ferocious Indians like Sitting Bull and Crazy Horse roamed, left an indelible impression upon my mind."

Still further west, in California, Italians made other contributions to music. As early as 1851 the Pellegrini Opera Troupe presented Bellini's *La sonnambula* at San Francisco's Adelphi Theater. By 1854 that city, where about half of California's Italian population was to cluster, boasted several opera companies. Under the management of P. T. Barnum, Eliza Biscaccianti (known as "The American Thrush") was enthusiastically received. In 1854 alone, 11 opera productions were staged in San Francisco. During California's early mining years a particular favorite was Gaetano Donizetti's *Daughter of the Regiment*, which received more performances than any other opera. In 1861 Madame Biscaccianti came back to the scene of her triumphs and tried to establish a local opera company. When she met with scant success, she took to drink and was reduced to singing in the Bella Union Saloon, where customers did not mind if she leaned unsteadily against a wall or table. In the 1860s the Bianchi Opera Company presented the California premieres of Gounod's *Faust* and Verdi's *Un Ballo in Maschera.* The Golden Gate also attracted the composer Pietro Mascagni as well as the divas Louisa Tetrazzini and the already mentioned Madame Adelina Patti.

She touched off what came to be known as the "Patti epidemic." Born in 1843, Adelina was the daughter of Salvatore Patti, a Sicilian singer and impresario. Madame Patti's first appearance in San Francisco in 1884 was preceded by an elaborate press build-up. When she sang a Bellini, Verdi, or Rossini opera, San Francisco went mad over her. Crowds followed her carriage or waited at the stage door to cheer when she appeared. Photographs of her adorned shop-window displays of opera cloaks for the "Patti season" as did Patti-style painted fans, lace handkerchiefs, pearl opera glasses, and opera bags. Hundreds of people were unable to gain admission to her performances. Because of the crowds that extended for blocks outside the ticket office, Patti's impresario once was fined $75 for violating a city ordinance that forbade obstructing traffic. She demanded what few other sopranos could—an aggravating delay before the curtain went up, during which she meticulously counted her fee of $5000, paid in full preceding each performance. These ended with the traditional singing of "Home Sweet Home." Her farewell tours were repeated annually for years.

The enjoyment of opera spurred some Americans to study Italian. In New York, as early as 1747, private academies offered instruction in the language. The first Italian in an institution of academic standing was Carlo Bellini. Mazzei introduced Bellini to Jefferson and, like Mazzei, Bellini involved himself in the independence struggle. In 1779 Bellini taught foreign languages at the College of William and Mary in Virginia.

By 1806, as the study of Italian became more popular, Da Ponte regularly taught it in New York. In 1825 he was appointed Professor of Italian Language and Literature at Columbia University. Da Ponte had critics as well as admirers. He was a braggart, yet he was well educated. Da Ponte shared his heritage with scores of pupils and friends.

Some early teachers were political exiles. One of these was Eusebio Valli, a medical pioneer, and a forerunner of Pasteur. In 1816 Valli came to North America, hoping to develop a vaccination technique against yellow fever. He arrived with a letter of introduction to Jefferson from the historian Carlo Botta. Jefferson entertained Valli at Monticello, where he explained his theories about the origin of yellow fever. Later, in Cuba, Valli injected himself with its bacilli and became a voluntary victim of the disease so he could test his vaccine, which proved effective.

Scientific contacts between Italy and America had begun during colonial days. Indeed, Italian books on scientific subjects were in the libraries of the Pilgrim fathers. A few colonials were graduates in physics from the University of Padua. Galileo corresponded with John Winthrop, who had traveled in Italy before 1629. Franklin, too, could read Italian and he corresponded with scholars like Cesare Beccaria. The American Philosophical Society included Italians as members. On a practical level, also, Italian technology was reasonably active. Illustrative of this was Giuseppe Taglialine who in 1831 came to New York and began manufacturing thermometers and other delicate instruments. The G. J. Taglialine Manufacturing Company ("Instruments for Indicating, Recording, and Controlling") is still in operation.

Antonio Meucci is considered by some historians of science to be the actual inventor of the telephone. A self-made scientist, he came to this country in 1850. After constructing several instruments, through which he and his friends spoke, he tried unsuccessfully to attract financial backing for his invention. When Alexander Graham Bell introduced the telephone publicly, Meucci claimed prior rights to the patent. A stormy dispute followed over which man had invented the device.

America's largest museum, the Metropolitan Museum of Art in New York, developed partly through the efforts of another controversial entrepreneur, Luigi Palma di Cesnola, soldier, diplomat, and the Metropolitan's first director. In 1860 Cesnola journeyed to New York, where he supported himself by giving French and Italian lessons. When the Civil War broke out, he volunteered his services to the Union Army. President Lincoln gave Cesnola an honorary commission as a Brigadier General, and later appointed him American Consul to Cyprus. While there, Cesnola studied early writings and maps by which he unearthed various forgotten archaeological sites.

In an age when each discovery fired the popular imagination, national museums vied for wealthy patrons to help them acquire ancient treasures. Cesnola became more interested in archaeology than in consular duties. His personal collection of antiquities grew so large that he transported it to England, announcing its availability for sale. Cesnola had read about plans for a new American museum and sold his collection at a reduced price to the new Metropolitan Museum of New York. This purchase gave the infant museum an impressive reputation. After Cesnola supervised the uncrating of his many artifacts, he returned to the Cyprus diggings to write a book about Cypriote history and his explorations. He was later elected Secretary of the Metropolitan Museum, a post which he held for life. As the museum's first head, he supervised the move to its permanent home in Central Park. The initial success of the Metropolitan is due in large measure to his devotion. Although autocratic and sometimes less than scrupulous, Cesnola had a knack for getting things done. As a result of his cultivation of American millionaires, the Metropolitan became a "gentleman's club" which received art treasures amounting to millions of dollars. From 1879 to 1904, the opportunistic Cesnola played a big role in the leadership of the New York art world.

America, land of immigrants, was fortunate to enjoy the talents of foreigners who became important in the development of its arts, education, and science. The culture which they transplanted helped soften the roughness of life in the New World.

Chapter Four Bibliography

For this chapter on Italians and early culture, the two books by Schiavo are again useful. The Pisani book and the one by Iorizzo and Mondello, as well as

The Federal Writers' Project's *The Italians of New York* should be consulted. Neil Harris discusses early culture in America in *The Artist in American Society, The Formative Years 1790–1860* (New York, 1966), as does Lillian B. Miller in *Patrons and Patriotism, The Encouragement of the Fine Arts in the United States, 1790–1860* (Chicago, 1966).

Marinacci's book deals with Brumidi (pp. 56–73) and Cesnola (pp. 74–94). Consult also Elizabeth McFadden, *The Glitter and the Gold: A Spirited Account of the Metropolitan Museum of Art's First Director, the Audacious and High-Handed Luigi Palma Di Cesnola* (New York, 1971). For culture in the West, see a series of monographs prepared by the Works Project Administration. One volume is entitled *The Italian Theatre in San Francisco* (San Francisco, 1939). Also consult Ronald L. Davis, *A History of Opera in the American West* (Englewood Cliffs, N.J., 1965). Hermann Klein, *The Reign of Patti* (London, 1920), describes Patti's popularity; see also Rolle's *The Immigrant Upraised* on the Italians out West.

Chapter Five

Italian Travelers

The new nation that had defied mighty England intrigued foreign scientists, artists, explorers, and traders. These independent spirits were drawn to America also for its natural splendors. One adventurer, Count Francesco dal Verme of Milan, simply wanted to see the new country and to meet its leaders. After visiting George Washington in 1783, dal Verme traveled to Yale College where he received an honorary degree. When the count returned to Milan he was a host to Jefferson, who came to see how cheese was made and how Lombardy's fine rice was processed in the Po River Valley.

Another nobleman, Count Luigi Castiglioni, naturalist and member of the Philosophical Society of Philadelphia, visited each of the 13 states. Upon his return to Italy, Castiglioni published a two-volume work on natural resources and plant life of America.

Another Milanese, Count Paolo Andreani, traveled to the American frontier. His interests were primarily scientific. In 1783 Andreani had made one of the first European balloon ascensions. In the summer of 1791 he explored the Lake Superior region and made observations to test whether the earth was a true sphere, a much debated subject. Andreani was probably the first white man to circumnavigate Lake Superior, traveling via birch canoe. His measurements of latitude and longitude seem to have been accurate. Like Castiglioni and dal Verme, he called upon Washington and Jefferson. For Washington he brought a copy of the Italian poet Vittorio Alfieri's "Ode to America." Much taken with the western theme, Andreani offered to prepare a description of his observations in Louisiana before Lewis and Clark's explorations. He, however, made some abusive remarks about Americans which aroused Washington's ire. Andreani's presence in the West as early as 1791 fits into the pattern of those foreign observers, drawn toward the outer fringes of North American settlement, who by their writings and experiences attracted others to follow.

Among the most picturesque of early foreigners to appear in America was a proud and haughty middle-aged Italian. This upperclass foreigner looked strange in buckskins, moccasins, and a soft felt hat. He was Giacomo Constantino Beltrami, who would call himself the discoverer of the source of the Mississippi River. Beltrami was more than six feet tall, of commanding appearance, proud of bearing, and quick to anger. A native of Bergamo, Beltrami came to America in 1823, a recalcitrant political exile of the Napoleonic Wars. As an increasing number of persons spilled over the Alleghenies into the Mississippi Valley, America's wilderness became his consuming interest. Beltrami was probably the first Italian to venture as far west as the Dakotas.

Travelers into virgin territory often attached themselves to official expeditions or joined parties of fur trappers in order to insure their personal safety. Beltrami, therefore, asked to accompany Major Stephen H. Long's United States topographical expedition from Fort Saint Anthony (later Fort Snelling, Minnesota) as far as Pembina in present-day North Dakota. Of all the earliest governmental expeditions yet to explore the region west of Lake Superior, Major Long's was the most important. Beltrami appreciated the opportunity to accompany this party, but fell into a serious argument with Major Long. The Italian angrily struck out on his own with the help of several friendly Chippewa and Ojibway Indians, discovering various remote lakes and rivers in what is now Minnesota. Beltrami, also a linguist and jurist, ultimately wrote the earliest geographical descriptions of that state's Red Lake and Turtle Lake area. At the mouth of the Thief River he made the mistake of dispensing with the services of his Indian interpreter. Soon thereafter a party of hostile Sioux attacked. One of the Ojibways was wounded and his Indian companions deserted Beltrami. The Italian, inept at canoeing, quickly tired, upsetting and drenching his provisions. After days of grueling travel, Beltrami made a series of portages southward to a sparkling lake. He named it Lake Julia for the Countess Giulia Medici Spada. Beltrami called the Turtle River the Mississippi, believing Lake Julia to be the source of the great "Father of Waters."

Beltrami emerged from the wilderness at Fort Saint Anthony. His head was "covered with the bark of a tree, formed into the shape of a hat and sewed with threads of bark." His outer clothing was composed entirely of "skins sewed together by thread made of the muscles of animals." Going down the Mississippi by keelboat, he reached New Orleans, sure that he had made the definitive discovery of the headwaters of America's major river. But he became embroiled in a controversy that lasted for the rest of his life after publishing a volume entitled *The Discovery of the Sources of the Mississippi and of the Bloody River* (1824). He had written harshly of Major Long and various prominent explorers. Long's own account retaliated, calling Beltrami's observations inaccurate and misleading. In 1832 Henry Rowe Schoolcraft, a naturalist and Indian authority, announced that *he* had discovered the real source of the Mississippi, a lake which he named Itasca. Beltrami's writings aroused so much interest that they influenced François René de Chateaubriand and James Fenimore Cooper, who based descriptions of Indians and frontiersmen upon his observations.

After Beltrami's death in 1855 his native Bergamo honored him as a great explorer and called him "the true discoverer of the sources of the Mississippi." A United States Geological Survey report at that time also credited Beltrami with this distinction. In Minnesota a county in the northern part of the state bears his name. An island in Lake Agassiz is also named after him, as is Lake Beltrami. Despite his temperament and the controversy that raged around him, Beltrami was more than a follower of other men's trails.

Another traveler who visited the American interior was Count Francesco Arese. He described his adventures in a book entitled *A Trip to the Prairies and in the Interior of North America* (1838). Arese, a Napoleonic sympathizer, arrived in the United States as an exile. In 1837 he undertook a trip up the Missouri River to what is now western Iowa, near Council Bluffs. From the Iowa region he traveled on horseback and by canoe into the Vermillion River country of present-day South Dakota. Like Beltrami, he ventured through the land of the Sioux and into today's southwestern Minnesota to Fort Snelling. Travel west of Saint Louis was still exceedingly rough, indeed sometimes dangerous; yet Arese made a unique 6000 mile trip ending in Quebec.

Italian journalists, exiles, and adventurers were struck by the contrasts of the American West. The writer Antonio Gallenga, who traveled into Nashville and Louisville in 1838, saw a paradox between its hills covered with oak, ash, and cedar forests and the American tendency toward wastefulness: "The Americans were soon to outstrip the very worst savages in Europe in their senseless and ruthless devastation of trees." He saw patches of Indian corn growing to heights that he had never seen in his own country. Gallenga also found the majesty of the land in stark contrast to the uncouthness of spittoon-using frontiersmen. Yet the sheer wonder of America's open countryside could not but impress most foreigners.

Books and letters about America circulated widely in Italy. How did these travel accounts picture the country? First it was big, very big. Travelers reported that beyond the Missouri the monotonous roll of the Great Plains, flecked with buffalo grass and mesquite, extended into the forested valleys of the Rocky Mountain chain. When newcomers reached the Omaha region, they were on the edge of an arid frontier in which Indians were hostile to them. In 1863 the Italian geologist Giovanni Capellini sought to describe his trip into this vast land of plains and rivers. Capellini was a professor at the Universities of Genoa and Bologna. An early exponent of Darwinian ideas, he had done significant work as a paleontologist, helping to establish the discipline of prehistoric archaeology. Capellini casually sauntered into the offices of Omaha's newspaper, the *Nebraskian*, seeking old issues of the paper with which to wrap fossil specimens. The next morning he was startled to read a full account of his life, hailing him as a significant figure in the interpretation of the West's geology. Capellini, pleased to believe that he was already well known on the frontier, commented most favorably on the degree of cultural awareness beyond the Mississippi in his book *Memories of a Scientific Voyage* (1867).

One of the most amusing of such travel accounts was *A Trip to the American Far West* (1881) by Giovanni Vigna del Ferro, who was in the United States for four years beginning in 1876. Vigna del Ferro obtained train tickets from the railroad financier Jay Gould and left for the West on a train with a troupe of actresses, including the celebrated Sarah Bernhardt. On the high plains, del Ferro found the "noble Indians" reduced to drunken sots, the buffalo largely decimated, and the prairies covered with the carcasses of steers. From Omaha onward, del Ferro deplored the cooking. Instead of whetting his appetite, western foods made him sick. He was glad he had brought along a chest containing wine, cans of tuna, mortadella, cheese, sardines, and butter.

After visiting Cheyenne, Denver, and Leadville, del Ferro camped in southern Colorado and northern New Mexico. He disapproved strongly of the extermination of the Indians and, in fact, applauded their fighting back—as in Custer's last stand—a most unpopular view at this time. He visited Apache camps along the Rio Grande, giving the Indians whiskey which they called "water of the devil." On the muddy streets of the mining camp at Leadville, del Ferro found a ratio of 30 men to one woman. He recorded the presence of only a few Italians working in the mines. He believed Leadville would not grow, because the town was more than 10,000 feet in elevation, and he thought domestic animals, including dogs, could not live there. He spoke of pneumonia as the order of the day and revolvers as the order of the night. Next, del Ferro and his party visited Salt Lake City and its Mormon Tabernacle, as well as Virginia City and Reno in Nevada Territory, and then San Francisco. His dispatches were reprinted in the New York newspaper *La Patria.*

Such travelers referred to the popularity of Italian opera throughout the American West. Modern historians, too, have commented upon the underestimated place of culture on the far western frontier, a subject related to the immigrant story. Foreign travelers like Carlo Gardini, for example, challenged the conventional view of life beyond the mountains. Far from stressing the primitive and material aspects of the West, they called attention to communities in which some persons read widely and also supported performances of plays and musical events. Sarah Bernhardt, members of the Booth family, as well as the Italian performers Salvini and Ristori met appreciative audiences throughout the West.

Travel accounts by foreigners almost invariably dwelt upon the Indians ("*i pelli rossi*"), the variety and grandeur of the country, as well as dramatic adventures they experienced. A book that conforms to a pattern we might call the "foreign western" is L. Simonin's *The Far West of the United States, Its Pioneers and Redskins* (1876). The author visited the United States five times between 1859 and 1875, filling his notebooks with descriptions of white massacres on the plains, raging prairie fires, buffalo hunts, revolvers, Indian funeral pyres, scalpings, and the intriguing plural marriages of the Mormons.

The most flamboyant and arrogant of all Italian travelers to the West was the patriotic exile and cosmopolite Colonel Leonetto Cipriani. A mustachioed nobleman six feet four inches tall, he was obsessed with romantic notions of glory and conquest. In his *Adventures of My Life*, published long after his death, Cipriani records that he bought cattle and surveying instruments to accomplish "a personal railroad survey of the West." In 1853 his caravan left Saint Louis with 24 men, 12 wagons, 500 cattle, 600 oxen, 60 horses, and 40 mules.

After a trek over the plains that lasted almost six months and which included an insufferable diet of beans and flapjacks, visits with the Mormons, Indian encounters, as well as stampedes, he finally got his caravan to California.

Cipriani found it inexcusable that the commandant of Fort Kearney sold him barrels of rotten flour and other unusable supplies. When he reached Chimney Rock—a resting place for parties on the Oregon Trail—he refused to carve his name on its base because so many American names were already there. He did, however, chisel his name and the following inscription on "Solitary Tower Rock": "Colonello Leonetto Cipriani—16 Luglio, 1853—Tiberio's tomb—Roman St. Angelo Castle—Tiber River" because the site reminded him of Castel Sant 'Angelo in Rome. In 1865, long after he returned to Italy, Cipriani was appointed a senator. In 1871 he retraced his earlier covered wagon route across America by Pullman car. Cipriani died in 1888 at his Italian castle.

One of the fullest late nineteenth century accounts was that of Francesco Varvaro Pojero who wrote *A Romp in the New World* (1876). An author of adventure stories, Varvaro had read de Tocqueville's and Dickens' travel accounts. He too was critical, even flip, about much of what he saw. Educated critics like Varvaro were not enthusiastic about a land where there was almost too much democracy and lack of manners. But Varvaro did approve of directness in law enforcement. He applauded vigilante action in the absence of law. At Canyon City, Colorado, a lynching taught him, he wrote, that Americans were intolerant of slow-paced legalities and that they did not believe in shielding criminals.

The background of such a traveler bore little resemblance to that of the immigrants he encountered. This was one reason they could not settle permanently in the New World. Educated foreigners were a peculiarity and they found it difficult to habituate themselves to the crudities of America. What they wanted to see was the country's geographical grandeur—Niagara Falls, the Grand Canyon, and the Canadian Rockies.

Earlier, Richard Henry Dana's classic account of pastoral California, *Two Years before the Mast* (1840), described his encounter with Italian seamen in its southern coastal waters. He saw a large boat near San Pedro filled with Italians "in blue jackets, scarlet caps, and various-colored underclothes, bound ashore on liberty . . . singing beautiful Italian boat songs all the way in fine, full chorus." Among the songs, Dana recognized *O pescator dell'onda*. Still later he ran across "three or four Italian sailors mounted and riding up and down the beach on the hard sand at a furious rate" as well as dancing in the nearby town. Almost every time an Italian boat went ashore it was, Dana said, "filled with men gaily dressed singing their *barcarollas*."

The earliest full description of California by an Italian is by Paolo Emilio Botta, son of historian Carlo Botta. Young Botta was in California during 1827, early in its history as a Mexican province. His vivid account of the sleepy pastoral province is entitled *A Voyage 'Round the World, Principally to California and to the Sandwich Islands* (1841).

Italian vessels arrived in California waters loaded with huge blocks of Carrara marble which their captains sold to defray the expenses of their voyage. Among the early ships were the *Flaminio Agazini* (1825), the *Rosa* (1834), and the *Citta di Genova* (1837). By 1850 so many Italians had arrived in San Francisco that Sardinia opened a consulate there in 1850, with Leonetto Cipriani the first Sardinian Consul.

During the California Gold Rush, incidentally, the enterprising Cipriani imported into San Francisco a house of some 1200 separate parts, assembled by 700 hooks and 26,000 screws. Unfortunately for him, Cipriani was dissuaded by Italians already there from buying San Francisco land for $12,000 which later in the nineteenth century sold for $200,000. After two years of service Cipriani found the position of consul in such conflict with his financial operations that he resigned. He sold his San Francisco property, including the Italian-made house, and returned east via Panama. On subsequent voyages to America, Cipriani engaged in mining and stock raising, buying and selling several ranches. During the Civil War he allegedly offered President Lincoln a plan to kidnap Confederate General Pierre Beauregard. Cipriani's successor as consular secretary (but never consul) was Federico Biesta, a lawyer who in 1859 helped to start San Francisco's *L'Eco della Patria*, the first Italian newspaper west of the Mississippi.

Americans, generally, are little aware of the accounts of these early Italian travelers. Europeans gained much of their knowledge of the New World from such observers. As we shall see later, letters by early immigrants also stirred a desire in the hearts of Italians to leave their homeland.

Chapter Five Bibliography

Books on Italian travelers are Schiavo's *Four Centuries of Italian–American History* as well as his *Italians in America before the Civil War*, Rolle's *The Immigrant Upraised* and Andrew Joseph Torielli, *Italian Opinion on America as Revealed by Italian Travelers, 1850–1900* (Cambridge, 1941).

Regarding dal Verme, consult *Seeing America and Its Great Men: The Journals & Letters of Count Francesco dal Verme, 1783–1784*, translated and edited by Elizabeth Cometti (Charlottesville, 1969). On Castiglioni, see Howard R. Marraro, "Count Luigi Castiglioni, an Early Traveller to Virginia (1785–1786)," *Virginia Magazine of History and Biography*, 58 (October 1950). About Andreani consult G. H. Smith, "Count Andreani, A Forgotten Traveler," *Minnesota History*, 19 (March 1938).

Writings about Beltrami include: Theodore Christianson, "The Long and Beltrami Explorations in Minnesota . . . ," *Minnesota History Bulletin*, 5 (November 1923), 249–264; Warren Upham, *Minnesota in Three Centuries*, 4 vols. (St. Paul, 1908)—the section on Beltrami is in Vol. I, pp. 372–375; G. C. Beltrami, *A Pilgrimage in Europe and America* . . . , 2 vols. (London, 1828); Luigi Villari, *Gli Italiani negli Stati Uniti* (Rome, 1939); and Roger C. Kennedy, *Men on the Moving Frontier* (Palo Alto, 1969).

For the travelers' own accounts of their journeys, see: *A Trip to the Prairies and in the Interior of North America, 1837–1838*, translated and edited by Andrew Evans (New York, 1934) as well as Lynn M. Case, "The Middle West in 1837, Translations from the Notes of an Italian Count, Francesco Arese," *Mississippi Valley Historical Review*, 20 (December 1933), 381–399. Concerning Gallenga, see his *Antonio Gallenga, Episodes of My Second Life; English and American Experiences* (Philadelphia, 1885). For Vigna del Ferro, consult R. G. Thwaites, ed., *Early Western Travels*, Volume 10 (Cleveland, 1904–1907). For Cipriani, see Ernest Falbo, trans. and ed., *California and Overland Diaries of Count Leonetto Cipriani from 1853 through 1871* (Portland, 1962) and Leonetto Cipriani, *Avventure della mia vita*, 2 vols. (Bologna, 1934). For Varvaro, consult Francesco Varvaro Pojero, *Avventure del nuovo mondo*, 2 vols. (Milan, 1876).

Chapter Six

Missionaries

Columbus took along an Italian priest on board the *Santa Maria* during his discovery voyage. This first member of a clerical vanguard went to the New World a full century before Englishmen landed at either Jamestown or Plymouth Rock. While the Spanish King's conquistadores relentlessly pursued gold, missionaries worked with equal zealousness to save souls and to bring their own brand of order to the wilderness. Priests of various nationalities were involved in the process by which Spain asserted sovereignty over North America from the sixteenth to the eighteenth centuries. Although under the flag of another nation, these clerics were dressed in the robes of a church which claimed universality. The already mentioned Marcos de Niza and Eusebio Kino were more than missionaries. They were important also as explorers and founders of missions.

The Kino legacy was followed by that of an inspector of Jesuit missions in Sonora and Sinaloa, Juan María de Salvatierra (or Salvaterra), a Milanese. In 1697 he founded the first of Lower California's missions at Loreto. He also established the celebrated Pious Fund to support continued missionary activity. In 1704 Salvatierra became Provincial of the Society of Jesus in New Spain and ultimately founded seven missions.

Associated with Salvatierra were the Sicilian fathers Francesco María Piccolo and Francesco Saverio Saetta. The latter was slain by the Pima Indians in 1695. Piccolo founded three more missions in Lower California. In working among the tribes of the Southwest some of these men met death, either at the hands of natives or by starvation and exposure. During a great Indian rebellion of 1680, 21 missionaries and several hundred Spaniards were killed.

The French, too, had Italian missionaries with them in the early days of colonization. At Quebec the Jesuit Father Bressani was captured by the Iroquois and was sold twice thereafter. Later he wrote an account of the Indian torture he underwent for the sake of religion.

In 1767, after King Charles III expelled the Jesuits from Spain's overseas provinces, some of them fled to Italy as exiles. One of the most learned men in the Jesuit order, the Mexican-born Francisco Clavigero, retired to Cesena, where he published a four-volume Italian-language *Ancient History of Mexico* (1780) and *History of California* (1789). Such books were useful in recruiting Franciscan friars to carry on the work of the Jesuits in America. Leaving behind a homeland that was among Europe's most picturesque, these men of God went unescorted among the heathen.

Not every priest who came to the New World labored in the wilderness. The first and only Catholic chaplain of the Congress of the United States, Dr. Charles Constantine Pise, was born in 1801 in Maryland, the son of an Italian father and an American mother. Ordained in 1825, Pise joined the faculties of Georgetown and Mount St. Mary's colleges. From 1849 to his death he was at the church of St. Charles Borromeo in Brooklyn Heights. (The first church for Italians in New York City, St. Anthony, was founded in . 866.) Aside from the honor of being chaplain of the Senate, Pise was a novelist, poet, and a historian of sorts. He attempted to offset anti-Catholic sentiment at a time when foreign priests were pictured as immoral and anti-American.

Father Pise had attended Georgetown College (later Georgetown University) in Washington, D.C. It was presided over from 1812 to 1816 by Father Giovanni Grossi, a native of Bergamo. Out of a small school Grossi created the first Catholic university in the United States. Italian Jesuits also established the College of the Sacred Heart at Woodstock, Maryland. The man who conceived what became Woodstock College was Father Angelo M. Paresce, a native of Naples who came to America in 1845. Because of the political situation in Italy in 1848, Italian "black robes" immigrated to the United States to become teachers of linguistics, the sciences, history, ethics, and canon law.

One of the first whites to study Indian languages was Father Samuel Mazzuchelli who, in the 1830s, left a wealthy Roman family to roam the plains and forests of Iowa, Illinois, and Wisconsin, as a Dominican priest. Mazzuchelli came to be known as Father Kelly by Irish parishioners. He published an almanac in Chippewa and wrote the first volume produced in the Sioux language. For years he was the only priest from the waters of Lake Huron and Lake Michigan to the Mississippi River. The design of the old State Capitol Building in Iowa City is attributed to Mazzuchelli.

Headed by Father Felix de Andreis, a Piedmontese, a group of Lazarist priests landed in Baltimore in 1816 and walked westward to Pittsburgh. Traveling down the Ohio River by flatboat to Kentucky, they reached Perryville, 80 miles south of Saint Louis, in 18. 7. There they built the Seminary of Saint Mary, a rough-hewn log establishment that combined training divinity students with farm chores.

In 1820, Father Giuseppe Rosati succeeded de Andreis as Lazarist Superior in America. Next Rosati became coadjutor bishop of Louisiana, then bishop of Saint Louis. This post entailed supervision of religious activities from Arkansas and Missouri to the Rocky Mountains. Under Rosati's patronage, the Jesuits founded Saint Louis University in 1829. He also founded the first school for deafmutes west of the Mississippi in 1839 as well as Saint Louis Hospital. Besides supervising the erection of Saint Louis Cathedral, Rosati started 34 churches in Missouri as well as convents, schools, and orphan asylums throughout the Mississippi Valley.

Bishop Rosati authorized the Belgian Jesuit Pierre Jean De Smet to found still more missions, schools, and parishes throughout the Rocky Mountains and Oregon Territory. After Indians from western Montana traveled eastward to Saint Louis in search of "the white man's book of heaven," Father De Smet made his 1840 journey to the tribes beyond the Rocky Mountains. Following that trip, De Smet returned to Saint Louis to appeal for added volunteers with which to Christianize the northwestern tribes.

From Italy, eager young Jesuits responded to De Smet's call. By 1841, the first of these, a 29-year-old Roman named Gregorio Mengarini, reported to De Smet at Saint Louis. That year De Smet, Mengarini, and their party traveled westward out of Missouri. Near an Indian village on the Kaw River they were joined by a party of about 50 immigrants, the Bidwell–Bartleson group (the first organized party to cross the Great Plains to California). De Smet guided them on the trip across the plains and over the Rockies. The Jesuit equipment consisted of four two-wheeled carts and a wagon drawn by mules. The priests themselves rode saddle horses. At a cutoff in present-day Idaho, Fathers De Smet and Mengarini bade the group farewell. Traveling on beyond the Snake River, the Jesuits headed into western Montana.

In its Bitter Root Valley, where the Flatheads lived, they built a crude log building chinked with clay. They named the place Saint Mary's. This was not only Montana's first mission and church; it became a point of departure for further missionary activity. De Smet left Mengarini in charge of Saint Mary's for the next ten years. Mengarini grew adept at the Selish and Kalispel languages. A basic source concerning the history of "Old Oregon" is Mengarini's *Narrative of the Rockies* . . . (1938). He also became the foremost authority on the language and culture of the Flatheads, publishing *A Selish or Flat-Head Grammar* (1861), printed in Latin and never superseded. These clerics sought to convert the Indians by speaking and using missals in the Indians' native language.

From 1841 to 1850 Mengarini founded other missions, taught catechism, organized an Indian band, played games with the natives, studied their folklore, and practiced medicine among them. It seems remarkable that a European could adapt himself to life in a wilderness. Mengarini and De Smet were in the tradition of Father Kino in the Southwest when it was a Spanish frontier more than a century and a half before.

Another Jesuit recruited by De Smet was Anthony Ravalli, a native of Ferrara. In . 844 he landed at Fort Vancouver and was to spend the rest of his life in the West. Having entered the Jesuit order at 15, he studied surgery, art, and the natural sciences. He was Montana's first physician and druggist. Father Ravalli could handle a plane, a foot adze, a carpenter's saw, and a dress stone; he could lay bricks, make furniture, set a horseshoe, as well as forge and temper iron. He made his own candles and was a good musician and painter. Furthermore, Ravalli was jovial and outgoing. His shortcomings were difficulty in learning various Indian dialects and laxity in maintaining discipline among the natives.

After 1845 Ravalli built Saint Mary's, a wooden structure 90 feet long and 60 feet high, completely without nails. He fashioned virtually every article necessary for church ceremonies. Ravalli transported a set of European buhrstones 300 miles by pack horse, to build Montana's first water-powered grist mill. Previously, both priests and Indians had existed on dried buffalo meat, fish, roots, berries, and a few vegetables. Aided by Father Mengarini, Ravalli also constructed a primitive sawmill and a still to extract alcohol from the camas root and sugar out of potatoes. In a small log dispensary he vaccinated Indians, performed amputations, and concocted medicines out of crude materials. These self-exiled clerics received mail from their homeland about once a year. They had to send Indians 800 miles to Fort Vancouver for provisions.

From 1860 to 1863 Ravalli was assigned to the Jesuit College in Santa Clara, California (Mengarini became its President). Ravalli returned to western Montana in the mid-1860s, where he ministered to gold miners. By the late 1860s, whites were also entering Idaho's panhandle area in great numbers. Ravalli, in boots and a long overcoat, with a breviary in his pocket and medicines and surgical instruments in his saddlebags, became a familiar figure who rode an Indian pony to visit the sick and injured. For 40 years Ravalli carried on his labors. Once, when asked if he ever felt the desire to return to Italy, he answered, "Yes, and I could have had that pleasure. But then the sacrifice would not have been complete." Ravalli County and Ravalli, Montana, a station on the Northern Pacific Railroad, were named in his honor.

Three of the six Italians listed in the first Oregon census of 1850 were Jesuits. The best known of these was Father John Nobili, a Roman who arrived in 1844. For five years he worked among Indians and trappers of the Hudson's Bay Company in "the Oregon country." Virtually alone among eight or nine thousand Indians speaking different languages, Nobili won the respect of the Hudson's Bay trappers by his devotion to duty. During a virulent epidemic that broke out among the Nesqually River Indians, Nobili persuaded them to renounce their custom of burning their dead and torturing surviving wives and husbands. Similarly, he got the Chilcotins to abolish polygamy. Nobili lived on herbs and roots supplemented when possible with horse, dog, or wolf meat. In 1849, when his health failed, he had to be ordered out of the Northwest. In California, he helped found Santa Clara College.

The career of another Piedmontese further illustrates Jesuit influence in the Northwest. This was Father Giuseppe Giorda, born of a noble Torinese family. In 1865 Giorda visited one of the wildest of western mining towns, Virginia City, after founding Saint Peter's Mission on the Missouri River and working among the Coeur d'Alene Indians. He hoped to establish a church at Virginia City. An atmosphere of violence and lawlessness highlighted the need for religion. During the Christmas season of 1865, Giorda attempted to find a chapel in which to celebrate mass. The priest was on the verge of abandoning his efforts when unexpected help came to him.

On Christmas Eve, news of Giorda's unsuccessful attempts to find space reached a local barroom. Several of its leading customers, raising their glasses high, contacted the forceful Irish governor of Montana, General Thomas Francis Meagher. The Governor helped collect gold so that Father Giorda could rent a theater. Virginia City's citizens transformed it into a church by removing all gaudy pictures and signs, hoisting a cross over the door, and bringing decorative evergreens into the building. The midnight mass that followed was so crowded that worshipers knelt at the door. As the former theater's proprietor complained that his building had been ruined for future use, Governor Meagher asked him to set a price on the structure. Then Meagher took up another collection. When the Governor handed the proceeds to the amazed Giorda, the priest burst into tears. The mass he had celebrated introduced Montanans to their first parish church.

Subsequently Giorda was chosen Chaplain of the Montana Territorial Legislature. From 1862 to 1866 he went on to become Superior Provincial of Montana's Jesuits. Refusing a bishopric offered by Pope Pius IX, Giorda continued to preach sermons in six Indian languages. The Indians called him "Roman Head." At Saint Ignatius Mission, Giorda helped Mengarini bring out his Kalispel dictionary and, with Father Joseph Bandini, published *Narratives from the Holy Scripture in Kalispel* (1879).

In the last stages of establishing missions in the Northwest, one more leader deserves mention. This was Father Joseph Cataldo, who had to leave Palermo with 90 other Jesuits after Garibaldi exiled the order from Sicily. In 1863 he traveled to California by sea and taught briefly at Santa Clara College. Two years later Cataldo went to the Jesuit Rocky Mountain missions. Cataldo was to spend the next 63 years with the Indians. From 1865 to 1928 he was active in Idaho, Washington, Montana, Oregon, Wyoming, and Alaska, mastering 20 languages. In 1877 Cataldo got into trouble with local Protestants and government officials over whether Chief Joseph of the Nez Perces should return to a government reservation. Cataldo acted as a peacemaker in the Nez Perce War that year with Father Ravalli. They exerted every effort to keep the Bitteroot Flatheads peaceful. Cataldo was known among the Indians as "Kaoushin," or Broken Leg. In 1881 he was the founder of Gonzaga University in Spokane as well as (until 1893) Superior General of the Jesuit missions in the Northwest, including Alaska. Cataldo Mission at Cataldo, Idaho, perpetuates his name. He died in 1928 at the age of 92, an honored man.

The wooden Italian missions with their white interiors that dotted the American Northwest reflected the cultural pattern from which their founders had come. These buildings were rough on the outside but delicate within. The Cataldo Mission, Saint Mary's, and Saint Ignatius in Montana represent the tangible results of a far-flung missionary system similar to the Spanish California mission chain of adobe and brick. Ultimately, parish churches were built near them, but these carefully wrought, rustic chapels were the first stage of a system created by dedicated men. One chapel still survives at Cataldo, Idaho.

Italian clerics were also active in the high mesa lands and deserts of the American Southwest. Although the dominant characteristics of its tradition were Spanish, Friar Marcos, Friar Kino, and other Italian priests had explored the region centuries before. In 1865 the Sisters of Charity, a teaching and nursing order, arrived at Santa Fe, New Mexico. This was still a dangerous frontier. Some notion of the problems these sisters confronted appears in the narrative of a Ligurian nun, Sister Blandina Segale. Her fascinating reminiscences, *At the End of the Santa Fe Trail* (1948), tell of meeting Billy the Kid while traveling by stagecoach to Santa Fe:

"Please put your revolvers away," I said in a voice which was neither begging nor aggressive. Spontaneously the weapons went under cover. The light patter of hoofs could be heard as they drew near the carriage opening. As the rider came from the rear of the vehicle, he first caught sight of the two gentlemen in the front seat, which gave me a chance to look at him before he saw us. I shifted my big bonnet so that when he did look, he could see the Sisters. . . . Our eyes met; he raised his large-brimmed hat with a wave and a bow, looked his recognition, fairly flew a distance of about three rods, and then stopped to give us some of his wonderful antics on broncho maneuvers. The rider was the famous "Billy the Kid."

Sister Blandina extracted a promise that she and her associates would be protected from further attacks by Billy's gang.

Her co-workers ultimately built a hospital for railroad laborers in New Mexico, a trade school for Indians, and various churches. They operated a quarry, processed their own lime, ran a brick-yard, opened lumber mills, ministered to the Apaches, and tried to end lynch law.

In 1867 the New Mexico sisters were joined by a group of Neapolitan Jesuits from southern Colorado, some of whom had also been expelled from Italy by Garibaldi. After the bishop of Santa Fe, John Lamy (about whom Willa Cather wrote *Death Comes to the Archbishop*), had gone to Rome to explain his pressing needs, a small group of priests and brothers were assigned to New Mexico. Bishop Lamy led Donato Gasparri, Rafael Bianchi, Livio Vigilante, Rafael La Vezza, and Prisco Caso from the East Coast via Fort Leavenworth by wagon and carriage.

Gasparri's narrative traces their journey into the Southwest. Along the Arkansas River, whose banks he described as "infested with Indians," they came across many "signs of destruction, such as houses in ruins, earth piled up over dead bodies, parts of corpses, arms, clothes, and abandoned wagons." One morning the priests, horror-stricken, "saw a band of 12 Indians, well armed and well provided." But they were surprised when the Indians "asked us for coffee and tobacco, and they in turn offered us buffalo meat." Although the Italians were not among the overland parties attacked by Indians, they lost several drivers and a nun because of cholera. The party finally reached Santa Fe on August 15, 1867, after traveling 7340 miles.

Gasparri and his associates were to minister to the Navajos and other tribes as well as to whites. They built schools, churches, and missions from the valleys of the Rio Grande northward into Colorado from Pueblo to Denver. In 1875 they founded the *Revista Catolica,* which became a leading Spanish-language journal of the Southwest.

California, a focal point for missionary activity, was more like home than was the American Southwest. Probably the first description of California and Oregon by an Italian was the missionary Louis Rossi's *Six Years in America, California, and Oregon* (1863). Two other missionaries, Fathers Nobili and Accolti, had established Santa Clara College in 1851. A considerable number of Italian northwestern Jesuits ended their ministries in California, 113 of these priests remaining there by 1879. Among them were Fathers Mengarini, Ravalli, Cataldo, and Giorda.

In the 1870s Dominic Giacobbi worked with Fathers Aloysius Varsi and Nicholas Congiato, the Presidents of Santa Clara College and Saint Ignatius College in San Francisco. Later, at the Novitiate of the Sacred Heart in Los Gatos, Giacobbi began growing wine grapes with the help of Father Congiato. This led to the production of the Novitiate's black muscat dessert wine, still sold today.

Father Anthony Maraschi, after teaching at Holy Cross and Loyola colleges in Baltimore, founded Saint Ignatius College (later the University of San Francisco) in 1855. One of its earliest professors was Father Joseph M. Neri, a Jesuit priest-inventor who, in 1874, devised a lighting system for exhibition and lecture purposes that utilized carbon lights. Neri's experiments occurred about ten years before Thomas Alva Edison's invention of the incandescent lamp. In 1874 Father Neri installed in the tower of the college a searchlight whose rays could be seen for 200 miles. Neri employed large batteries, then magnetic machines, and finally dynamos. He utilized California's first storage battery and magnetic electric machine. In 1876 Neri illuminated San Francisco's Market Street by using three arc lamps of his own invention.

Those priests and nuns who had faced the rawness of the frontier, from Montana to Lower California, might well have remembered Donizetti's lines:

> Oh, Italia, Italia beloved
> Land of beauty and sunlight and song!
> Tho' afar from thy bright skies removed,
> Still our fond hearts for thee ever long!

Isolated from their homeland, the missionary impulse was not easily understood by the loved ones whom some of these clerics had left behind forever.

Chapter Six Bibliography

Books with information on Italian missionaries in America include Schiavo, *Four Centuries* and his *Italians in America before the Civil War*; Rolle, *The Immigrant Upraised*; Bolton, *Rim of Christendom*; Peter M. Dunne, *Pioneer Black Robes on the West Coast* (Berkeley, 1940); and Wilfred Schoenberg's books, *Jesuits in Montana 1840–1960* (Portland, 1960) and *Jesuits in Oregon, 1844–1959* (Portland, 1959).

On Salvatierra, see Miguel Venegas, *Juan Maria de Salvatierra*, translated and edited by Margaret Eyer Wilbur (Cleveland, 1929); on Mazzuchelli, see his *The Memoirs of Father Samuel Mazzuchelli, O.P.* (Wilmington, Delaware, 1967); about Rosati, see Robert F. Trisco, *The Holy See and the Nascent Church in the Middle Western States, 1826–1850* (Rome, 1964).

For Mengarini, Ravalli, Giorda, and Cataldo, see Albert J. Partoll, ed., "Mengarini's Narrative of the Rockies . . . ," *Sources of Northwest History*, Number 25 (Missoula, 1938), a pamphlet; Robert I. Burns, *The Jesuits and the Indian Wars of the Northwest* (New Haven, 1966); H. M. Chittenden and A. T. Richardson, eds., *Life, Letters and Travels of Father Pierre-Jean De Smet, S.J.,*

1801–1873, Volume 2 (New York, 1905); L. B. Palladino, *Indian and White in the Northwest; Or a History of Catholicity in Montana* (Baltimore, 1894); George F. Weibel, *Rev. Joseph M. Cataldo, S.J., A Short Sketch of a Wonderful Career* (Spokane, 1928).

For Southwestern missionaries see Blandina Segale, *At the End of the Santa Fe Trail* (Milwaukee, 1948) and D. M. Gasparri, "Account of the First Jesuit Missionary Journey across the Plains to Santa Fe," *Mid-America*, 20 (January 1938), 57–58.

Chapter Seven

Before the Crowding Began

In 1850 there were fewer than 5000 Italian residents in the United States. The political disorders that followed the European revolutions of 1848 had forced some to flee to nearby England rather than across the Atlantic. Most of these refugees hoped for an opportunity to return home. Only a few made the trip to distant America. By 1860, nevertheless, its Italian population had reached 10,000, and in 1880 the Italians numbered just under 50,000.

New York's Italian colony began to come alive in those years, strengthened by musicians, artists, and merchants. Lorenzo da Ponte's memoirs indicate that political exiles exchanged their rifles for English grammar books. A few taught Italian. Most of these immigrants settled in a section of New York named Five Points. Only later did Mulberry Street evolve into that city's "Little Italy."

The most famous of these refugees was Garibaldi himself. He lived on Staten Island for a time, and molded candles on Bleeker Street for the inventor Antonio Meucci. The majority of refugees, unlike Garibaldi, lost hope of changing political and social conditions in their old country. Reconciling themselves to life in America, they became citizens. Since these immigrants were few in number, there was little unemployment, and, thus, they experienced relatively little prejudice.

Political refugees who wanted to retain their military traditions joined an Italian-trained guard in New York. Others organized a branch of Giuseppe Mazzini's "Young Italy" organization. In 1849 Chevalier Secchi de Casali founded *L'Eco d'Italia*, the first Italian newspaper in the United States. A disciple of Mazzini and comrade of Garibaldi, Casali kept exiles informed about conditions in their native country. By the 1860s his paper stressed the improvement of immigrant welfare in America. Casali also sponsored a night school for Italian children at Five Points. In 1857 he and other immigrant leaders formed the Society of Italian Union and Fraternity, which included a library and a night school for adults.

The Italian government and the Vatican were both anxious for the perpetuation of Catholicism among immigrants who had gone to America. In 1866, in order to offset the influence of its many Protestant churches, the parish of Saint Anthony of Padua was founded on Manhattan's Lower West Side. Two years before that the first Italian Catholic parish had been created in Hoboken, New Jersey. By 1875, Philadelphia, Newark, and Boston also had Italian Catholic congregations.

On the eve of the Civil War, *L'Eco d'Italia* encouraged the formation of an Italian Legion, to be commanded by Italian officers. Exiles who had fought for a united Italy now volunteered to face death for the American Union. Colonel L. W. Tinelli led such a regiment under the banner of the Garibaldi Guard at the battle of Bull Run, at Harper's Ferry, and at Gettysburg. When the Civil War broke out, Francis B. Spinola of New York offered to raise another brigade of volunteers. Although a staunch Democrat, he encouraged others to forget their differences and to unite behind Lincoln. For his services in recruiting Italians, Spinola was commissioned a Brigadier General. Twice wounded, he became a state senator and later a member of the United States Congress. During the war, President Lincoln also gave Luigi di Cesnola an honorary commission as a Brigadier General. You will recall that Cesnola later became the American Consul to Cyprus and after that Director of New York's Metropolitan Museum.

In the first year of the Civil War, Lincoln offered Garibaldi, who had considered taking out American citizenship papers, a major-generalship in the Union Army. By 1860, however, Garibaldi was deeply involved in planning Italy's liberation movement. Had his first duty not been to his own country, he would probably have fought with the Union forces.

On the East Coast a few early Italians made a special impact. Paolo Busti is considered by some to be the founder of Buffalo in New York state. He became the general agent of the Holland Land Company, and under his direction the surveying and development of the northern part of New York state was carried out. In 1832, Marquis Niccolo Reggio arrived in Boston. He was of Genoese family origins but was born in Smyrna. As Boston was a center for the importation of Mediterranean products, especially fruits and wines, he became an importer. Reggio had seven vessels carrying dried fruits and other delicacies from the Mediterranean to both North and South America. He fell into a fierce rivalry with an Armenian, Joseph I. Iasagi, for Boston's Mediterranean trade. When Iasagi had a statue to Aristides erected in the city's Louisburg Square, Reggio proceeded to erect one to Christopher Columbus.

Chicago's Italian residents grew from 100 in 1860 to 4091 in 1884. At first, these Italians tended to settle in family groups. The men had little difficulty finding good jobs. Originally, Italians settled mainly south of the river in the Loop district. This area later became a financial center, and those who owned real estate there prospered by moving to Chicago's suburbs. The city contained relatively few blocks with a solid Italian residency; even its "Italian districts" were only 50 percent Italian. "Little Italys" also developed in Philadelphia and Rochester.

During the years before mass immigration, fishermen, farmers, soldiers, and political figures took up permanent residence in former Spanish and French Louisiana. In 1796, François Marie Reggio became the royal standard bearer of the New Orleans *cabildo,* or town council. Venetian Giovanni Gradenigo presided over the trustees of the Church of the Immaculate Conception at Opelousas. Peter Sarpy navigated the first keelboat on the Missouri River. He and his brother, John B. Sarpy, were associated in the 1840s with both the Missouri Fur Company and the American Fur Company at Saint Louis. Louisiana's earliest Italians became so rapidly assimilated with the French and Spanish that they virtually lost their ethnic identity, some even changing their names.

One finds Italians associated with a variety of pursuits in early Louisiana. In the medical profession, Doctor Francesco Antommarchi of New Orleans became Napoleon's personal physician on the island of Saint Helena. Captain Salvatore Pizzati, born in Sicily in 1833, arrived in New Orleans on the eve of the Civil War and grew wealthy importing fruit from Central America. In the 1880s he sold a flotilla of vessels to the United Fruit Company for a handsome profit. Pizzati also operated a brewery, an insurance company, and a 14,000-acre plantation. After the turn of the century, toward the end of Pizzati's life, he built and endowed a New Orleans orphanage to care for destitute Italian waifs. In his lifetime, he was one of the wealthiest Italians in the United States.

Italians who lived in the South fought with the Confederacy during the Civil War. Experiencing property damage, they appealed to Italian authorities in gaining compensation from the United States government. When officials in Washington refused responsibility, however, this strained diplomatic relations with Italy. Casali's New York newspaper warned that Italians should not continue with a divided allegiance: they could not be Italian and American at the same time.

Italian laborers, unable to pay $40 per acre for swampy or forest-covered land, worked on a share basis not unlike the *Mezzeria* system of Tuscany. Under this scheme, landowners assigned families to separate tracts, furnishing tenants seeds and tools. Each cultivator was expected to till a few acres of vegetables. At the end of the growing season, part of the produce was credited to him and part to a landlord who deducted rent or other advances until the sharecropper became a landowner. Slowly Italians in the American South bought up land abandoned by others. Digging drainage canals, they converted sticky mud bogs into tillable farm soil. In Arkansas and Louisiana former sharecroppers raised sugar cane, corn, strawberries, peaches, and apples, seeking to master both climate and competition.

In Texas during the first half of the nineteenth century, there were few foreigners besides Spaniards. However, some Italians became prominent. Angelo Navarro, a Corsican, was one of the founders of San Antonio in 1777. One of the first Texas land commissioners was his son José Antonio Navarro, a member of the convention which declared Texas independent of Mexico. Other Italians participated in the Texas Revolution. The Marchese di Santangel was one of Sam Houston's most loyal adherents, operating a press at New Orleans through which he lashed out fiercely at the Mexicans.

A curiously named Italian, Decimus et Ultimus Barziza (called "tenth and last" by his father), went to Texas before the Civil War. He came from a titled Venetian family which had settled at Williamsburg, Virginia. Barziza, a graduate of William and Mary College, became a Confederate captain with General Hood's Fourth Texas Infantry. He was taken prisoner at the battle of Gettysburg. Afterwards he became a criminal lawyer and was elected to the Texas House of Representatives.

By 1860 an acre of farmland in the Midwest cost about $16. To raise cash Italians worked in such towns as Des Moines, Sioux City, Davenport, and Council Bluffs. They bought property in and around these communities and eventually acquired the expensive machinery needed to become successful farmers.

Although Italians were not, in general, strongly attracted to the Midwest, by 1880 they made up one-third of the population of Iowa's Hamilton County. The federal census that year showed that almost half the farmers in that county were foreign-born. Italians established a newspaper, the Des Moines *Tribuna Italiana*, and influenced the naming of Iowa towns and counties: Aetna, Mount Aetna, Como, Florence, Garibaldi, Genoa, Genoa Bluff, Milan, Palermo, Paoli, Parma, Turin, Verona, Marengo, and Verdi.

In Nebraska by 1863, an Italian colony had clustered around the outskirts of Omaha. Single men working on the Union Pacific Railroad lived in boarding houses, and families moved into a district called "Dago Hill," located near other immigrant areas, among them "Sheelytown," "Polack Hill," and "Little Bohemia," where they owned lunchrooms, stores, and vegetable gardens.

Still farther west, Salt Lake City and the Mormons aroused great curiosity abroad. Few foreign travelers failed to include Deseret Territory in their itineraries or descriptions of their travels. Although the Mormons coaxed only a few permanent Italian residents there, they actively recruited converts. In 1849 Lorenzo Snow, ordained as one of "Mormonia's" Twelve Apostles, left for Italy with Joseph Taranto (or Toronto). Taranto, a native of Sicily, had given Brigham Young his savings of $2500 to help build the Mormon temple at Nauvoo, Illinois. Snow and Taranto sought converts in Genoa, Italy, and in its provinces of Liguria and Piedmont. On October 19, 1850 they ascended a mountain outside Genoa where they offered prayer and, as if to turn the tables on the American West, formally pronounced the peninsula of Italy as a missionary field. In Italy, Elder Snow wrote a tract entitled *The Voice of Joseph*. During 1852 he also published the book of Mormon in Italian. By 1855 the three branches of the church in Italy had sent a bare 50 converts to America while only 64 others made up the membership in Italy. Most of these were Protestant Vaudois of the Waldensian persuasion.

In 1866, seventeen Vaudois families reached Salt Lake City. Later, more of them settled there and at Ogden. Immigrants sorely missed their Alpine homeland, its fresh milk, cheeses, wines, chestnuts, and fruits. At times they were reduced to eating weeds, roseberries, and bran. Grasshoppers consumed crops and dust clogged the immigrants' nostrils.

The Mormons, eager to attract converts, were frequently kind to foreigners. Leonetto Cipriani, the Italian aristocrat who traveled through Salt Lake City in 1853, was touched by the friendship shown him by a Neapolitan music teacher, Gennaro Capone. Another musician, Captain Domenico Ballo, Salt Lake City's first bandmaster, headed an instrumental band which had blown its way across the plains.

Richard Burton, the English adventurer, came to the Great Basin in 1860, gathering notes for his *The City of the Saints.* By 1875 Burton's book was translated into Italian, an indication that Mormon recruiting in Italy had stirred up increased interest. Foreigners were fascinated by polygamy but did not fully understand the requirements of Mormonism. They could be excommunicated for religious negligence and "general immorality."

South of Deseret lay Colorado, which first attracted miners from mountainous Liguria. In 1859 four Genoese, the Garbarino brothers, started out for the Rocky Mountains. During the spring of that year, attracted by rumors of gold and loaded with mining implements, they accompanied an ox-train that left Saint Louis. One of the brothers, Charles, settled down in what was then a brawling mining camp, the site of today's Golden, Colorado. Two other brothers, Joseph and Antonio, wandered around other camps, finally reaching Georgetown in 1860. The fourth brother, Louis, made his home at Boulder. By 1870 the Garbarinos had earned enough from mining to send for still another brother.

There is no record of an Italian in all of Oregon from the time of the early Malaspina expedition until 1827. That year, Captain Giovanni Dominis led the brig *Owyhee* into the Columbia River; it was one of a handful of ships to reach that coast so early. Dominis spent two weeks carefully navigating the treacherous river, sounding its bottom as he collected a precious cargo of furs for the China trade. In 1829 Dominis returned to the Columbia in search of a new cargo of furs. On this trip he conceived the notion of curing quantities of river salmon. He returned to Boston with 53 barrels of this precious fish. Although it had cost him little, Dominis' cargo did not reap the rewards that he had expected because the United States government taxed the shipment as a foreign import. Yet the *Owyhee* began a large trade in salted salmon between the East and West Coasts of the

United States. Dominis was also the first man to plant peach trees in Oregon; from California he imported sheep, and throughout the 1830s he collected sea otter furs on the Northwest coast in exchange for rum.

Another Italian in early-day Oregon was S. N. Arrigoni. He was a Milanese who landed in Portland in 1856 while wandering around the world with a new Irish wife. Along the banks of the Willamette, Arrigoni founded a hostelry which he named "The Pioneer." As Portland's first hotel of note, it became a 300-bed establishment. Arrigoni invited famous people to his hotel, including Generals Ulysses S. Grant and William Tecumseh Sherman. This hostelry, and another called "Arrigoni's," provided guests with the first telegraph and express service in Oregon. Arrigoni gave Portland its first streetlight, a small oil lamp which stood outside his hotel. Upon his death in 1869, Arrigoni was considered one of Oregon's most appreciated pioneers.

The California Gold Rush attracted many nationalities, including Italians. In 1851, New York's *L'Eco d'Italia* reported that there were already more than 600 Italians in San Francisco alone and approximately 6,000 in California. Abandoning their ships to search for gold in the Mother Lode country, Italians named one mining area "Italian Bar," just as the Mormons had called their diggings "Mormon Bar."

One of the Gold Rush arrivals was Domenico Ghirardelli, who became prosperous primarily because he did *not* seek the elusive gold of the Sierra. Instead, he traveled through California's mining towns selling chocolates and hard candies called *caramele*. At San Francisco his factory, begun in 1851, manufactured both liqueurs and chocolates. After his death in Rapallo, Italy, in 1894, his heirs continued to operate the Ghirardelli Chocolate Company, today in Ghirardelli Square.

Other Italians were successful in the Sierra mining camps. A storekeeper, Mastro Gagliardo, did business at the rate of $5000 per day at Mariposa. The ruins of stores and hotels run by Italians dot California's mountainous interior. In 1858 some 300 lonesome miners, loaded with gifts, walked nine miles to welcome the first Italian woman ever to travel into the California mining area.

Some California Italians went into ranching and dairying. A man named Tresconi raised 40,000 cattle on a quarter million acres near Monterey. Alessandro Repetto, a Genoese, purchased a 5000-acre rancho after the Civil War. He raised sheep and cattle there for almost 20 years. In 1885 he died, leaving the rancho to his brother Antonio, who preferred to live in Italy and who came to California only long enough to sell the rancho for $100,000. This area later developed into Montebello, a town east of Los Angeles.

After the Comstock mining strike of 1859, miners from California went to nearby Nevada. A sprinkling of Italians helped to carve out mining shafts and tunnels in its Comstock Lode. A Signor Crosetta operated a saloon at Virginia City as early as 1861. Its Molinelli Hotel, which dates from the same year, still stands. In October 1870, the Italian residents of Virginia City held a dinner to celebrate the unification of Italy. *L'Eco d'Italia* pointed out that numerous Italians had also settled at Treasure City, Nevada. The federal census of 1870 confirms that, except for one butcher, the Italians at this mining camp were mule packers, miners, charcoal burners, ore smelters, or quartz millers.

In 1864, in part because of the shortage of miners during the Civil War and because the demand for cheap labor remained strong, Congress passed an act to encourage the immigration of such laborers. Although rescinded four years later, there was no formal enforceable prohibition against continuing the search for labor in foreign countries. For decades, agents regularly sent manpower, under contract, to the United States.

Soon all this freedom and mobility would be tempered by a new mood. When, after the Civil War, America turned toward industrial growth, financial empires were built with little regard for the disadvantaged. Italians encountered discrimination, poor housing, and bad working conditions at the very time their numbers were increasing. As employers began to hire more Italians, they came into competition with Irish laborers. At that time, the Irish had more political strength than the Italians. Other Americans, too, seemed to search out scapegoats for the increasing violence in their midst, and the myth spread that Italians were violent and lawless.

Later immigrants were less skilled. Some were illiterate and uninstructed in the ways of American labor; the *padrone* system became for them an intermediate step to full assimilation. The *padrone,* or boss, was someone who spoke their language and who could contact American employers. This age-old method of work control resembled the seventeenth-century indentured servitude which had brought the earliest Englishmen to North America. The *padrone* system featured remnants of feudal serfdom originating in the Mediterranean world. In America the *padrone* recruited mining, railroading, and agricultural labor, negotiating contracts for the laborers he herded around in gangs.

The quest for "captive workers" persisted until 1885, when the importation of these contract laborers was finally ended by law. Contractors, taking advantage of widespread illiteracy, frequently sent former peasants, accustomed to meager fare and hard work, to the United States under exploitative conditions. Since they arrived in excessive numbers, foreigners were usually paid less than other workers. A self-serving *padrone,* in collusion with contractors, could easily take advantage of gullible and ignorant immigrants, binding them for up to seven-year work periods. The *padrone* furnished transportation to their place of work; he was the middleman who represented workers and employers to each other. His opportunities for corruption were, therefore, unusual. The *padrone* hired the immigrant (frequently in America without family) at a fixed rate and profited from whatever wage he obtained above that rate. In some cases he paid immigrants what he saw fit. He not only demanded commissions from both laborers and employers but made money out of furnishing them food; he could even exact a commission from wages which workers sent back to Europe; and he might also finagle a cut out of the steamship passage of those returning homeward.

The *padrone* system, however, was not solely a negative force; many immigrants would have been lost without such help. An ambitious few struck out on their own. Others used the middleman only for a few months. Honest *padroni* could help ghetto dwellers get out into smaller communities. The rural *padroni* often urged Italians to become citizens and to learn the new language. They provided such intermediary services as banking, letter writing, buying or selling property, and settling estates. The *padrone* system took over some of the functions of the old-world family system.

Secchi de Casali was one of the first American Italians to recognize the importance of directing Italians toward rural districts. In 1874 Casali obtained the sympathy of a large American landowner, Charles Landis. He put tracts of land in Vineland, New Jersey, at the disposal of Casali for the development of a colony. Landis visited Italy to recruit workers for the project. North Italians arrived first, buying uncleared land for $20 to $25 an acre. While the men worked at a nearby factory, their families picked berries and did other farm work. As farms were paid for, more terrain was purchased. By 1908 over 950 families owned land. The venture reached self-support in three years. Casali's newspaper used Vineland as an example of how Italians could manage without *padroni.* More such planned colonies would, indeed, have reduced the need for *padroni.*

From Vineland, New York, Chicago, Denver, and Sacramento, from little settlements and big ones, letters went back to Italy—scrawled in mining camps, railway stations, farm shacks, and tenement rooms. These letters, often with a money order inside, spread the contagion of immigration as no representative of a steamship company could do. The hope of finding work in America's mines, the promise of a railroad job, or of work building a subway, and the lure of farm land in the Midwest—these all helped to produce the mass immigration about to descend on America.

Chapter Seven Bibliography

Books helpful for understanding the period before mass emigration occurred include Schiavo's two volumes, *Four Centuries* and his *Italians in America before the Civil War*, and the Pisani book. Two books by Ella Lonn, *Foreigners in the Confederacy* (Chapel Hill, 1940) and *Foreigners in the Union Army and Navy* (Louisiana, 1951) deal with non-Americans during the Civil War period.

Information about Italians in Chicago before mass immigration is in Humbert S. Nelli, *Italians in Chicago, 1880–1930* (New York, 1970). See also Rolle, *The Immigrant Upraised*, regarding Italians in various Western states. For further research on Italians in Colorado, see Giovanni Perelli, *Colorado and the Italians in Colorado* (Denver, 1922). For California, see P. E. Botta, *Observations on the Inhabitants of California, 1827–1828* translated and edited by J. F. Bricca (Los Angeles, 1952). Ruth Teiser's *An Account of Domingo Ghirardelli and the Early Years of the Ghirardelli Company* (San Francisco, 1945) is helpful, as is H. F. Raup, "The Italian-Swiss in California," *California Historical Society Quarterly,* 30 (December 1951), 304–314.

A new interpretation of the *padrone* system is in Iorizzo and Mondello, *The Italian–Americans.*

Chapter Eight

The New Immigration and Urbanism

By the end of the nineteenth century, America was emerging as a powerful industrial country. The welcome mat was out to newcomers who could assist in its growth. Until after World War I, the major legal obstacle to free nondiscriminatory immigration was the Oriental Exclusion Act. Foreign-born laborers were to play a critical role in constructing railroads, subways, tunnels, bridges, and in supplying farm labor. Everywhere there was much to do in the prodigal land.

The new immigrants from southern and eastern Europe were strikingly different from previous immigrants in appearance, language, and customs. Some came only to save money and then to return home. Others, content to live in deprived industrial areas, showed little initial interest in American government or society. Four-fifths of them settled in eastern cities, nestling into pockets of individual nationalities.

The Italian usually came over alone or with a brother, son, or other male of working age. He borrowed money, worked aboard ship to pay for his passage, or was advanced funds by a *padrone*. Life in steerage was grim, lasting from a month to a minimum of two weeks, and was crowded and uncomfortable. Italians brought along knapsacks full of local cheese and salami to supplement the despicable soup and hardtack doled out to passengers. Lice, scurvy, and seasickness added to their misery. Friendships grew as the innocent sufferers helped each other. Passengers anxiously paced the decks or studied books "guaranteed" to teach English within the time of the voyage. Others consulted guidebooks that explained the strange money system and printed useful sentences in basic English, also warning newcomers about hazards at dockside.

After landing at New York or Boston the immigrant had to show proof that he would not become a public charge. Screening by the Italian government gave its migrants one of the lowest rejection rates. Yet, any unaccompanied young woman might be suspected of prostitution, especially if her hands were uncalloused by work. Physical examinations were devised to detect glaucoma and communicable diseases. Some immigrants considered these tests and the literacy tests that were required demeaning.

As many as 15,000 Italians passed through Ellis Island per day. The tempers of customs officials as well as of debarkees grew sharp under pressure. Misunderstanding and confusion reigned in the brick terminal sheds where future Americans had to be processed before they were allowed to debark on the mainland. Finally, amid the loud shouts of a strange language, immigrants were met by relatives, friends, or *padroni*. Others milled about the crowds at dockside with their names pinned to the lapels of their coats, clutching scraps of paper on which were scrawled strange addresses.

A few came to believe that America was hardly putting out a welcome mat. Loan sharks and boarding-house swindlers victimized unwary foreigners to such an extent that, after the turn of the century, the Society for the Protection of Italian Immigrants was formed to help them at dockside. The society's first secretary was Gino C. Speranza. In 1904, after he traveled to Italy and gained the sympathy of the Italian government, the organization sent volunteers to Ellis Island to help immigrants find relatives or friends. Speranza also took newcomers into New York and provided them with temporary lodging. His organization inspected living accommodations weekly, which prompted landowners to improve their property. Speranza's society also assisted Italians seeking employment, and it investigated conditions in labor camps across the country. Publicizing abuses led to remedial measures; eventually the society established schools in some camps.

By 1912 there were 258 Italian mutual aid societies in New York City alone. But most of these were weak, supported by nickel and dime contributions. Had American officials and social workers cooperated more closely with them and with Italian authorities, immigrants might have been encouraged to scatter instead of settling primarily in congested centers. At first their record in America's large cities was mixed. While income long remained low, Italians were never high on the pauper lists compiled by social workers. In 1904, for example, the Irish had the highest percentage of indigents among all foreign nationalities in the United States. The low Italian percentile is possibly due to the fact that men frequently came into the country specifically to work at a job which had been promised before departure from Italy. The 1904 records also revealed that the Italians did not, in any large numbers, become inmates of charitable institutions, such as orphanages, rescue missions, or old age homes. In 1904 the United States Bureau of Immigration listed the origins of foreign-born paupers in the following percentages:

Irish	30 percent
Germans	19 percent
English	8.5 percent
Italians	8 percent
Hebrews	8 percent

At that time, Jews and Italians contributed the same percentage of indigents to the welfare rolls. As for criminality, Italian arrests in Boston and Providence in 1904 formed a smaller percentage than that of any other foreign-born group.

Slowly, a new sense of community was awakened among former *paesani*. Being with people of one's own sort was important. Young Italian men, sensitive to ridicule, were slow to venture away from their countrymen in search of employment. Other factors encouraged the bunching of immigrants together. Industry was moving increasingly toward the cities. Isolated farm life in the United States contrasted sharply to Europe's gregarious rural villages. Some peasants, furthermore, rejected any sort of agricultural work; their memories of hardship and oppression in grubby rural settings were not always happy. The glowing lights of the city posed an alternative. The city also offered ready employment at wages above those which farmhands received, even in the United States.

In the "Little Italys" of the large cities, blocks were divided into sections of Sicilians, Genoese, or Calabrians. Italians were surrounded, thus, with others speaking their own dialects. Regional tradesmen satisfied every need for familiar foods and goods. But these "Little Italys" were not only ethnic ghettoes; their clannishness was based on provincial as well as national factors. In New York, Neapolitans and Calabrians composed most of the Mulberry Bend district; Genoese grouped themselves along Baxter Street; Sicilians were on

Elizabeth Street; west of Broadway there were Piedmontese and Lombards; and near the Hudson River on 69th Street Ticenese Italians settled. Each colony sought to preserve its folkways, demonstrating a slight distrust of persons from different sections of Italy. Gradually these attitudes receded as immigrant laborers mingled at work with one another and with native Americans. Regional dialects understood only by their own folk gave way to an improvised Italo-American jargon.

Gradually, the immigrants began to fit into their environment, changing it to suit their needs. Though income was low, women took a particular pride in bargaining with the Polish butcher or Yiddish fish peddler as well as with suppliers of Italian foods. Returning from marketing, oil-cloth bags stuffed with provisions, the family kitchen became a center for experimentation with new products. The growth of the Italo-American community expanded the need for food like that of the old country, especially wine, cheese, salami, and pastas. By the 1890s, those who had once made spaghetti and macaroni in family kitchens became the owners of small factories which sometimes expanded into larger food supply companies. Others saw different opportunities for business: New York was full of pushcart vendors who required little capital with which to begin selling fruits and vegetables from their own gardens or from those of friends. Beginning with such humble origins, the fruit trade on the East Coast came to be dominated by Italians.

On warm evenings, Mulberry Street came alive with playing children, pushcarts, baby carriages, strolling lovers, and gossiping neighbors seated on stone door stoops. For perhaps too many Italians, Mulberry Bend became America. Herded there by compatriots who had themselves only recently arrived, they lived in basements, garrets, outbuildings, and stables converted into dwellings.

In 1895, the Mulberry Bend area's level of sanitation was temporarily condemned by the city's board of health. Jacob Riis, among the most astute early commentators on immigrant life, described the zone as a veritable pigsty whose dark alleys were a favorite hiding place for criminals. Before Ellen Collins reconstructed several antiquated tenement houses on Mulberry Street and Water Street, some children rarely saw sunlight, even outside the hovels which formed their slum world. When Theodore Roosevelt became President of the New York Police Board, he shamed the city into planning Paradise Park. By 1909, children could play where the tenements of Bottle Alley and Bandit's Roost had once stood.

However vibrant the atmosphere, not all Italians wanted to live in a crowded, open-to-your-neighbor type of community. Some yearned for their own home surrounded by a piece of land on which they could grow fruit and vegetables. Wives encouraged their men to seek employment in labor camps, planning to follow them and leave New York City behind. Escaping Mulberry Bend, Italians moved into neighborhoods vacated by previous immigrant groups—just as Puerto Ricans and blacks would later supplant them on the Lower East Side. The immigrants who had "made good" left behind somewhat better tenement houses in Brooklyn, the Bronx, or on Long Island. The availability of work in these suburbs created the new "Little Italys" whose remnants still exist.

Both contractors and *padroni* tried to lure immigrants to other cities by promising better wages. Both were known to pocket fees, then to lead immigrants to lonely places and abandon them. Others were sent to areas where there was little housing. Transportation and maintenance costs, plus fees to *padroni,* left little for the foreigner to save. The *padroni* might advance travel expenses, but only at high rates of interest. Some ignorant immigrants were bound financially for years. Another device to bilk immigrants was the company store or commissary, located close to the labor camp. Debt-ridden Italians, forced to use the contractor's store, paid prices as high as 100 percent above cost to the seller, with quality as bad as the price was high.

Contracts signed in Europe were unenforceable in American courts. Once immigrants learned this, they tore up these agreements, which they had signed only in order to reach the New World. Or, the immigrant might run away from even a legal contract if labor conditions grew unendurable. Opposition voiced by the Italian government also helped to break down the controversial *padrone* system.

With the passage of the Foran Act in 1885, the *padrone* legally lost his ability to contract labor. As Italians became more Americanized and workers joined labor unions, they freed themselves from dependency. In 1896 a survey of Italians in Chicago showed that they worked for *padroni* less than three months after reaching America.

Newcomers could rarely get the jobs for which they were trained if they did not know English. Artisans sometimes dug coal or carried bricks. Laborers who showed ambition and who attended night classes in English were sooner able to start their own businesses or obtain skilled work. If an Italian had enough money to avoid using a *padrone,* he waited, hoping to get a job in his accustomed trade, whether as a mechanic, shoemaker, barber, musician or stonemason. Highly developed railway engineering in northern Italy had produced laborers who were used to tunneling under mountains; these men formed a labor pool for American railway and subway engineers. Indeed, more than 4000 Italian subway workers helped to dig the New York underground system. One of them, an intelligent youth named Salvatore Ninfo, organized a union among them. After he won better working conditions and higher pay for his men, other construction laborers demanded the same benefits.

Labor extended into family life, as was the tradition in Italy. As long as the law permitted it, thousands of women and children entered the garment trade and other factory employment under sweatshop conditions. Some took piecework home for little pay. Italians were unpopular because they displaced other laborers by accepting lower wages, thus lowering wages for other workers.

During the national depression of 1907, the influx of Italian shirtwaist makers coincided with a growing fad for more casual women's wear. These workers were nonunionized and willing to work part-time on a piecework basis. The result was the disruption of the unionization drive of the Jewish-led International Ladies Garment Workers Union of New York.

Employers sought to utilize foreign workers to threaten newly unionized labor. When Italians were used as strikebreakers they were either ignorant of what they were doing or there was little alternative, since unions barred some newcomers from joining. Discrimination, nevertheless, led them to band together in mutual aid societies. Italians admitted into the bricklayers', tailors', or stonemasons' unions sometimes moved back to their own societies, depending on what benefits they could gain. Italian is still spoken in a local of the ILGWU in New York's garment district.

Italian confectionary stores, meat markets, and art dealers dotted America's sprawling cities. From an early date, New York had two Italian newspapers, *L'Eco d'Italia* and *Il Republicano.* Protestants, under the auspices of the city's Children's Aid Society, ran missions and taught English as well as other skills. At one time there was only one Italian Catholic church to serve the entire city—San Antonio di Padua on Sullivan Street. Yet there were two Italian Protestant churches. Charlotte Adams wrote in *Harper's Monthly* that the notion of New York's Italians being "an idle and thriftless people is a superstition which times will remove from the American mind." After going to the city's Caffe Moretti, which foreign musicians and artists frequented, she observed: "In view of the general assimilation of Italians with their American surroundings it is surprising and delightful to find a place that retains so picturesque and Italian a flavor." This view changed as the influx grew.

By 1903 there were 1,200,000 Italians in the United States, 12 percent of whom lived in greater New York City. Its construction needs alone called for a vast army of laborers willing to work for relatively low wages. Walter Weyl wrote a vignette for *Outlook* entitled "The Italian Who Lived on Twenty-Six Cents a Day." Weyl featured a former peasant named Pacifico who "secured his dollar and fifty cents a day, minus railway fare, minus the arbitrary charge for the doctor, minus [the *padrone's*] fee, minus the exorbitant sums extorted for the rotten food Vincenzo sold him. Pacifico, born in a bottomless poverty, was not spoiled, and he shrugged his shoulders at the hard work, the bad food, and the ceaseless exactions. The essential fact remained; he earned a dollar and a half a day; he lived on twenty-six cents a day." When Pacifico began to earn more than $1.50 per day, he was released from the bonds of the *padrone*. He married, sent his children to school, and finally became economically independent. "A bank account today is what a log cabin and a hundred-acre lot were a hundred years ago," Weyl maintained.

Favorable appraisals of this sort were countered in the popular press by condemnatory articles. A Harvard professor, Robert Ward, wrote in *Outlook* during 1904: "The easier we make it for every undesirable immigrant to find work—and it is chiefly the undesirable ones that are crowded into our cities—the more we shall induce others to come; and, furthermore, the more we scatter our recent immigrants, the more widely do we spread the evils which result from exposing our own people to competition with the lower class of foreigners."

The United States Civil Service Commissioner emphasized certain advantages of mass immigration: "However undesirable, at a mere cursory glance, this large and constantly increasing stream of foreign immigration may appear, I am satisfied that, in the end, the coming to our shores of . . . the more adventurous part of the population of Italy is bound to add to the vigor of our race and to help keep it from decay." Other authors stressed the fact that there were then virtually no Italian tramps and little prostitution or crime. In 1906 inspectors of the New York Tenement House Department reported that its Italian quarter was crowded but cleaner than other foreign districts. Landlords considered Italians good tenants who paid their bills regularly.

Photographs taken in Mulberry Bend by a physician, I. W. Bart-
lett, at the end of the nineteenth century belie the squalid impression
that local newspapers gave. Poverty existed, but gaiety, too, was apparent. We have descriptions of music pouring from open windows
and of dozens of music shops where opera lovers could purchase the
latest Caruso or Gigli records.

What of the "Little Italys" elsewhere? Life in Rochester, New
York, may give the reader some notion of what they were like. Italians
still comprise the largest group of foreign-born in Rochester. A few of
them arrived as early as 1860. Most came after the 1870s and 1880s as
migrant laborers who knew little English, usually brought by a *padrone*. By 1889 Rochester's Italian tenement section was overcrowded
to such an extent that some civic-minded ladies organized an Italian
Mission. They began English classes and other instruction to give the
group a new "self-image." The Italians also organized their own societies. The first, called the Bersagliere La Marmora, was initiated by
persons who had obtained citizenship papers. Its members staged pic-
nics as well as balls and marched in Fourth of July parades. Other
ethnic groups included the Società Italiana, the West End Political
Club, and the Italian Columbia Military Band.

Newspapers in Rochester and elsewhere featured stories about an
Italian criminal organization, the Mafia, or Black Hand (*Mano Nera*).
Crime, then as now, touched the lives of few Italians directly but, unfairly, it affected many of them by association. Reporters attempted to
link local crime with the Mafia, searching for scapegoats in the Italian
colony. The murder, in 1890, of the New Orleans Police Chief increased public suspicion that Italians (and particularly Sicilians) were
behind other crimes. The yellow press fanned such suspicions. In
crowded tenements at Rochester and in other large cities, Italians
feared they would be accused of affiliations with hoodlums whom they
loathed. To replace the *padrone's* protection, a few fell back upon
knife or gun. Whenever violence flared up, local authorities wisely
began to hire patrolmen who could speak immigrant languages. By
1905, a group called the Italian Protection League protested linking
Italians with crime and supported the police in enforcing the ban
against concealed weapons. The group spearheaded a drive to clean
up Rochester's "Little Italy."

More than any other goal, Italians craved the stability that came
with obtaining American citizenship. Study groups and political clubs
that advanced this cause grew in popularity. Italians also began to celebrate their role as Americans. In 1909, the Cristoforo Colombo Soci-

ety staged a huge parade and picnic on the first Columbus Day celebrated in New York state. Thousands attended—Italians as well as
other residents. By this time the Italian community had reached almost 10,000. Gradually they gained acceptance and respect in Rochester.

Chicago had long attracted all nationalities, and no area was occupied exclusively by one ethnic group—except later in Negro districts. Although immigrants settled in distinct parts of the city, its Italian districts were less than 50 percent Italian. The closest
approximation to a "Little Italy" was located on the West Side, in the
vicinity of Hull House.

Social scientists and educators spoke out against injustices in the
American heartland. Some put pressure on the courts to protect immigrants as social workers took over problems that the *padroni* had once
handled. In 1909, Illinois passed legislation to protect immigrant laborers. All contracts henceforth had to be filed with the state and a
copy given to the worker. Fines and imprisonment were imposed on
unscrupulous employers.

Chicago came to be a center for seasonal jobs. Construction and
railroad workers went there to seek work. In the early 1900s the newly
arrived immigrants formed the bottom of its economic pay scale.
Some Italians never got beyond this unskilled stage. Gradually, however, they became grocers, barbers, shoemakers, bakers, blacksmiths,
druggists, painters, and even small factory owners. A 1913 survey revealed that only Jews outnumbered Italians in business ownership in
the Seventeenth Ward.

As Chicago's Italians became active in the labor movement, they
sometimes acted as strikebreakers, which earned them the hatred of
other workers. Oscar Durante, the owner-editor of Chicago's *L'Italia,*
urged immigrants not to succumb to the "enemies of labor" and to
join in striking against unfair working conditions. He also encouraged
them to obtain United States citizenship, as the Germans and Irish
had, and to participate in politics by forming a voting bloc. Ward
bosses needed cohorts who could speak the language of their constituents. For this reason, Johnny Lazia cooperated with Kansas City's political boss Thomas Pendergast and became the virtual czar of its
North Side.

Conditions for Italians in the Midwest did not vary greatly from
one city to another. In Milwaukee, for example, Italians had founded
a small colony in the 1880s near the Chicago and Northwestern Railroad yards. By 1915 there were 9000 of them in the city, 80 percent

from southern Italy. Because they knew too little English, they did menial jobs.

Social workers reported they had difficulty changing Italians' diets. Parents sometimes sent their children to school with only *caffe latte* (coffee mixed with milk) for breakfast. In Italy, schoolchildren return home at midday for a lunch of *pasta* and fruit. Immigrant mothers were not used to the American school lunch-bag routine. As Italians placed a high priority on food, not many of their children suffered nutritionally, yet some eager social workers sought to force other styles of eating on all immigrants, including Italians.

Other proposed cultural changes were resisted as well. Some immigrants, particularly Sicilians, hated courts and other governmental institutions, especially those involving the police. They felt only cowards went to court. In general, Italians wanted to care for their own needs. The Milwaukee colony produced 15 mutual benefit societies which also flourished in other cities where large numbers of Italians lived.

Whenever possible, ethnic politicos who could deliver bloc votes saw to it that patronage jobs filtered down to the Italian community. Boston's Italians competed with the Irish, who were more sophisticated politically. In a community controlled by Irish police and ward bosses, Italians assimilated less rapidly than they did elsewhere. In churches and other institutions, the Italians found it humiliating that the majority was Irish. Boston's San Marco Society was formed to establish a church for Italians only. Although its members raised funds to purchase a Baptist meetinghouse, the local Irish Archbishop refused to give them his benediction because the society insisted that it have control over funds. Finally, in 1890 after sympathetic ecclesiastics interceded at the Vatican, the church opened as the Sacred Heart Parish.

Boston's Italian quarter was virtually a closed city within a city. Its North Enders seemed neither Italian nor American in lifestyle. Before the turn of the century, several thousand of them engaged in fruit importing which linked them to each other. Yet, a sense of inferiority persisted among them.

This was not the case at San Francisco, whose North Beach was a world in itself. San Francisco's pasta factories produced miles of *tortellini* and *lasagne*. Imported Marsala bottles lay resplendent in the showcases of grocery stores. Bakeries on Columbus Avenue featured *grissini* and hard breads *al'Italiana*. At a restaurant like the Fior d' Italia one could order Milanese cutlets, *cioppino,* or *zabaglione*. On

Fisherman's Wharf, mariners mended their nets as they had done for generations at Leghorn or Genoa, propping up sagging spirits after an unsuccessful catch with straw-covered demijohns of red wine. A merchant could join the Camera di Commercio Italiana or put his money in the Banca Popolare. One could read *La Voce del Popolo* or *La Colonia Svizzera*. Italian physicians, lawyers, and bankers took care of basic needs. Confession in Italian was heard in two churches.

San Francisco's Washington Square and Los Angeles's North Broadway district, like their eastern counterparts, were crowded with yelling Italian children. Tomatoes and garlic dried in back yards. These sectors, however, seemed less cluttered, depressing, and confining than the Columbus Squares of the East. By 1880, the foreign-born constituted 34 percent of California's 864,694 inhabitants. Most of them clustered in San Francisco.

A western oasis of cosmopolitanism and of the arts, "the City" attracted Italian performers like Adelina Patti and Louisa Tetrazzini. Madam Tetrazzini returned from world trips to give numerous sentimental performances in San Francisco. Indeed, the city named a gourmet dish after her—Chicken Tetrazzini. The Metropolitan Opera Company made an annual tour to San Francisco. Tenor Enrico Caruso sang *Carmen* at the city's Grand Opera House on April 17, 1906. Later that night, the unforgettable earthquake and fire occurred. Caruso ran downstairs to the lobby of his hotel. He joined the throngs of people running toward Union Square to escape the danger of buildings collapsing on all sides along Market Street. When asked about his experiences that night, Caruso shouted: "Give me Vesuvius!"

Many other artists came to San Francisco. A member of the Naples San Carlo Opera Company, Gaetano Merola, organized the San Francisco Opera Association and was its director for 30 years. This is the second oldest continuous opera group in the nation. The Italian colony was large enough to support five daily Italian newspapers. Italians also began their annual Columbus Day pageant at San Francisco, still staged by the grandsons of Genoese and Sicilian fishermen.

Reservations about the future of immigrants persisted well beyond World War I. Were ethnically mixed peoples condemned to social disintegration as inferiors to be degraded by political ward bosses? The old *padrone* concept—that the leader of a group knew best what was good for his people—persisted until Italians lost some of their naiveté and saw the need to seek nonethnic acceptance. American authorities wondered, however, if immigrants could strike out on their own in any large numbers. Could they develop more wholesome and permanent relationships to the wider community beyond the bossism, *padroni,* and ward heelers who clung to them and to whom they were attached? Hardly recognized then was the psychological price the immigrant paid for losing his culture and native language as he attempted to move into the American system. Although today we may feel we have overcome the bigoted, untrusting attitude of former generations toward foreigners, many prejudices have persisted and influenced legislation regarding immigrants until recent times.

Chapter Eight Bibliography

Books particularly useful for the period of mass immigration are: Edward Corsi, *In the Shadow of Liberty* (New York, 1935); Herbert J. Gans, *The Urban Villagers, Group and Class in the Life of Italian–Americans* (New York, 1962); Nathan Glazer and Daniel P. Moynihan, *Beyond the Melting Pot, The Negroes, Puerto Ricans, Jews, Italians, and Irish of New York City* (Cambridge, 1963); Antonio Stella, *Some Aspects of Italian Immigration to the United States* (New York, 1924, reprinted in San Francisco, 1970); William Foote Whyte, *Street Corner Society: The Social Structure of an Italian Slum,* rev. ed. (Chicago, 1943); and Phyllis H. Williams, *South Italian Folkways in Europe and America: A Handbook for Social Workers, Visiting Nurses, School Teachers,* rev. ed. (New York, 1938, reprinted in New York, 1969). Previously mentioned volumes are: Federal Writer's Project, *The Italians of New York;* Iorizzo and Mondello, *The Italian–Americans;* Nelli, *Italians in Chicago;* Pisani, *The Italian in America;* Schiavo, *Four Centuries;* and Tomasi, et al., eds., *The Italian Experience.*

A representative list of articles dealing with Italians and the urban environment are: Charlotte Adams, "Italian Life in New York," *Harper's Monthly,* 62 (April 1881), 676–684; John Foster Carr, "The Coming of the Italian," *Outlook,* 82 (February 29, 1906), 419–431; Edward Corsi, "Our Italian Fellow-Americans," *American Mercury,* 55 (August 1942), 197–205; William E. Davenport, "The Italian Immigrant in America," *Outlook,* 73 (January 1903), 27–37; Norman Di Giovanni, "Tenements and Cadillacs," *Nation,* 1877 (December 13, 1958), 443–445; Blake McKelvey, "The Italians of Rochester: An Historical Review," *Rochester History,* 22 (October 1960), 1–23; "Mulberry Bend from 1897 to 1958, Pictorial Story," *Saturday Evening Post,* 231 (August 2, 1958), 34–35; Humbert S. Nelli, "Italians and Crime in Chicago: The Formative Years, 1890–1920," *American Journal of Sociology,* 124 (January 1969), 373–391; J. H. Senner, "Immigration From Italy," *North American Review,*

162 (May 1896), 649–657; Gino Speranza, "Solving the Immigration Problem," *Outlook,* 76 (April 16, 1904); and two articles by Walter E. Weyl, "The Call of America," *Outlook,* 94 (April 23, 1910), 883–890 and "The Italian Who Lived on Twenty-Six Cents a Day," *Outlook,* 93 (December 25, 1909), 966–975.

Chapter Nine

Onto the Land

Italians once engaged in agriculture were apt to consider living in an American metropolis as a step up the socioeconomic ladder, while others could never be content in the crowded city. From 1860 to 1900, almost 36 million immigrants swelled America's cities, and 9 million went to farms. But it took money to own land, and sending for relatives in Italy usually absorbed what little cash immigrants had saved. Visions of farm ownership usually came to nought.

At the turn of the century, American reformers maintained that the ills of the cities could be solved by sending foreigners to the countryside. They argued that, though farm workers might be poorer than city dwellers, they ate better and were happier. Journalists further pointed out that although Italians in the South were discriminated against in the cities, they were accepted more readily as farm laborers.

In 1901 the Italian Commissariat of Emigration, which regulated immigration, also suggested that Italians would be happier in rural America rather than in the cities. Baron Edmondo Mayor des Planches, Italian ambassador to the United States, toured America to determine where former *contadini,* or farmers, might best pool their resources. But he was unable to control where they settled, and they chose sites that ranged from excellent to hopeless.

Italian farm colonies were formed in various ways. Sometimes successful immigrants encouraged others to join them. In other cases, companies were set up to plan specific developments. In spite of careful planning and official support, some rural colonies came to nothing. In 1892, Alessandro Mastro-Valerio of Chicago founded an Italian agricultural colony at Daphne, Alabama. Although this venture received aid from Jane Addams and Hull House, Chicago Italians did not support the colony and it failed.

Other groups did succeed, however. Some rural pockets of Italians still exist. One of the oldest colonies is in Genoa, Wisconsin, begun with only eight families. They cleared the land, planted grain, and began dairying. In 1893, thirteen Waldensian families immigrated to another tract named Valdese in North Carolina on land purchased by the Waldensian religious sect. Because the soil was poor, they sold some of it and concentrated on growing grapes for wine as well as milling flour, cotton, and producing lumber. The Waldensians established yet another colony at Monnet, Missouri.

Immigrants who grew fruits and vegetables outside the large cities sometimes bought land collectively. The towns of Vineland and Hammonton, New Jersey, were begun this way. As growing grapes was a veritable way of life for Italians, it was natural that they should establish vineyards in the Hudson River Valley and Finger Lake district of New York as well as in California's San Joaquin, Sonoma, and Napa valleys. As soon as possible, they sought to control the land on which they subsequently established wineries. Former railroad workers and miners sometimes stayed on where their last work camp had disbanded, hoping to accumulate enough money to buy farmland.

While these immigrants marked time on the edges of rail centers or mining camps, they needed facilities and institutions once provided by the *padrone*. One of these was the boarding house. There, lonely men (the majority of them in their twenties) could relax amid familiar foods and language and the laughter and companionship of their *paesani*. Homes away from home, these establishments hosted Italians from many regions: Sicilians sang their ballads, and Piedmontese played *morra*, a finger guessing game. Others came to exchange information about jobs, news of the old country, and for relaxation from the day's work.

The record of Italians who settled outside large urban centers, whether in colonies or as individuals, stands in contrast to the notion that they formed a static, nonmobile, introverted group. Their success in agriculture makes it obvious that the role of city laborers has been overstressed in immigrant history.

The Italians transported old-world methods of cultivation to the New World. In Italy, *contadini* farmed in a highly structured way. They lived in small villages and went out daily to work their plots of land. Terrain was precious, and every available yard was cultivated.

Social life centered around friends and relatives in their village. Therefore, the extensive wheat farming of the Midwest was unfamiliar. America's farm families generally lived long distances from one another, but Italians preferred to remain small truck farmers, if only on vacant lots at the edge of towns. There they planted tomatoes, beans, or eggplants among fruit trees or between rows of berries, growing two or three crops at the same time. The immigrant's front yard, ordinarily used by Americans for flowers or a lawn, might also be planted with grapes or vegetables.

Whether he owned his land was the real test of a man's worth. Any sacrifice was endurable to reach that goal. See the following table for results of one study to determine percentage of ownership versus tenancy among Italian farmers.

Proportion of Italian Farm Owners to Italian Tenants in 1920

Region	Italian farm owners	Italian tenants	% of owners	% of tenants
West north central states	422	170	71.28	28.72
West south central states	1555	936	62.42	37.58
Mountain states	1576	304	83.83	16.17
Pacific states	3195	1703	65.23	34.77

Source: Edmund de S. Brunner, *Immigrant Farmers and Their Children* (New York, 1929), p. 4.

Bruno Roselli, an Italian journalist of the 1920s, considered it an act of courage for immigrants to leave the safety of the cities, however crowded, and urged Italians to make this move: "You are unsuccessful and unhappy here. You cannot compete in business with the Jew, while your ignorance of English puts you at a disadvantage with the Irishman. Get away from such competition, and let us see whether your strong arms will not bring abundant riches out of the soil. . . . You . . . lacked opportunities in Europe and [will fail] to find them here when in cities crowded with craftier peoples, but [may thrive] when facing the obstacles of nature."

One area that provided few opportunities was the American South. After the Civil War, the South seemed alien in every way. Even if the immigrant was a tradesman or artisan, the area offered him few opportunities to practice his skills. If he was a laborer, he became involved in the emotional struggle between white and black, which placed immigrants into competition with depressed labor in a climate quite unlike that of Europe. Immigrants were warned not to migrate into the South, advice which undoubtedly cut down their number.

Yet, the Southern states operated active immigration bureaus. Because farm workers increasingly left the land for city work, many farms were unable to survive and were sold. The days of slave labor were over and social friction had driven some black workers to the North. Therefore, these states offered special inducements to foreigners who would work on farms. Passage money was sent to bring *contadini* directly from Italy, and railroad companies offered grants for settlers. By 1885, the Yazoo Delta's first Italian agricultural colony was located at Friar's Point, Mississippi. Other Italians fanned out through Washington and Bolivar counties and westward across the Mississippi River.

Cosmopolitan Louisiana attracted more Italians than any other state west of the Mississippi River except California. There were direct sailings between Naples, Genoa, Palermo, and New Orleans. After the turn of the century the French market at New Orleans came to look more Sicilian than French. The state once boasted as many as five Italian newspapers. By 1910, Louisiana had more than 20,000 Italian-born residents, of whom some raised sugar cane and cotton as tenants or laborers on plantations.

A few Southern newspapers predicted that heavy Italian migration would displace Negro labor. A colony at Sunnyside, Arkansas, encouraged such notions because 500 immigrant families lived there in 1895. Austin Corbin, a Northern industrialist who owned the Long Island Railway, made this settlement financially possible. Instead of recruiting Italians from the big cities of the United States, Corbin and the Mayor of Rome agreed to transport immigrants directly to his colony. These workers were sent up the Mississippi by steamers of Corbin's Anchor Line. Bakers, tailors, and shoemakers fresh from Italy were dismayed when Corbin supplied them with agricultural implements, draft horses, seeds, carts, a railroad, a steamer, and cotton-bailing equipment, as well as a school, a church, and a telegraph office.

Corbin's venture was a mixture of humanitarianism and hard-nosed Yankee enterprise. Although his American foremen treated workers with a tyrannical attitude carried over from dealing with slaves, the Italians rose to the challenge of toil and heat, outproducing black cotton-choppers.

The experiment at Sunnyside throws light upon how Italians lived elsewhere. Their houses were covered with strings of dried butter beans, peppers, and sun-cured corn. Meat was a luxury. *"Per fare bella figura"* (to make a good showing), they dressed children neatly and kept their dwellings clean. In adjoining woodsheds, they kept firewood, sawed and ready for the winter months.

Sunnyside, however, was never well drained, and it remained dangerously malarial. Just as Corbin was about to provide for pure water and proper sanitation, he died. Settling his estate took so long that the project was jeopardized. Meanwhile, there was an alarming increase in the colony's mortality rate. During 1898, a majority of the Italians abandoned Sunnyside in panic. In the autumn of the next year, 80 colonists died within one month; others returned to Italy, while some moved to other states or to South America. Only 40 families remained. Had Corbin lived, this might have been one of the most successful experiments in American agricultural history.

Eventually a new leader arrived at the Sunnyside colony to minister to the immigrants. This was Pietro Bandini, a young Italian priest. Seeing the plight of his stranded countrymen, Father Bandini told them:

I have promised God that I would save you, and save you I will. Where is the coward who would balk at the difficulties? Where is the materialist who will whimper if he must go without food now and then, or sleep, as our ancestors did, under the starry heavens? You are my flock, and I, your God-given shepherd, will lead you into the sheepfold. Follow me at once.

Father Bandini arranged for the remaining colonists to buy land in Missouri and Arkansas. In 1898, after negotiating with the Saint Louis and San Francisco Railroad, he obtained an option on 900 acres of Ozark land in the northwest corner of Arkansas. The railroad sold the immigrants this terrain for only one dollar per acre. The colonists cut logs from the nearby forests and built homes there. Italy's Queen

Margherita sent funds for a church and Bandini helped to construct it. The priest imported seeds, tools, and even insect larvae to combat local pests.

After a few years of difficulty the Italians were successful in dairying, grape growing, and fruit raising. With their new leader making the arrangements, 50 families named the new community Tontitown in honor of Enrico Tonti (Henry Tonty), the symbolic "Father of Arkansas."

To finance buying more land for the colony, the immigrant men worked in local zinc mines and coal pits. Wages in these mines amounted to only one dollar for a 12-hour day. Added to low pay and cold quarters, the colonists encountered other difficulties. A cyclone destroyed their first crop of strawberries and vegetables, forcing them to live off *polenta,* or corn meal.

Tontitown experienced further difficulties. Inhospitable and resentful neighbors set fire to the Italians' schoolhouse. Infuriated, Father Bandini warned nativist raiders that sentinels would be placed on guard around the settlement. His threat made an appropriate impact.

Tontitown's Italians, studying United States Department of Agriculture reports, learned about crop rotation and scientific agriculture. An abundance of Concord grapes led the Welch's Grape Company to build a plant nearby. Three creameries, a broom factory, brickyard, blacksmith, and cobbler's shop further diversified commerce. Tontitown flavored the life of one of America's most noncosmopolitan states. Before his death, Bandini returned to Italy where he received the plaudits of the Pope, the Prime Minister, and the Queen Mother.

Minnesota's mines became another magnet for immigrants. By 1910 there were 10,000 Italians in Minnesota. Nearby, Michigan's ore-rich Keweenaw Peninsula, jutting out into Lake Superior, was also a mining center. Its copper production was transported to the outside world by way of the Sault Sainte Marie canal. Southward lay the Menominee and Gogebic iron ranges, among the richest in the world. Long before Detroit became an automobile center, this mining country provided employment for all nationalities.

America's railroads also vied for laborers. Recruiters for rail companies promised prospective settlers along their tracks that they would market crops, extend credit, and assume the functions of banks and colonization societies. Section hands liked to go where climate was warmest and where all-year employment could be found. But since this work consisted of long hours of setting rails and ties in sweltering heat or in the clammy drizzle of winter, other jobs lured transients away from manual labor at "track's end."

Trains then traveled over very uneven tracks. Long trips were an ordeal. Crowded immigrant cars were poorly designed for human traffic: hard wooden benches served as seats; straw pallets were laid out at night for sleeping; passengers washed in tin basins on the rear platform. At many a wayside station, overpriced snacks of smelly cheese, old eggs, and dry bread were all that was available. To unload at some water-tank railway station, immigrants would jump off, followed by bales of bedding, roped suitcases, bags of macaroni, salamies, and clanging bundles of cooking utensils. A mother might unload a baby carriage in the middle of a sandy vineyard or orchard as a heavy stove or pasta machine made its appearance at trackside.

The writer was once told how a young girl, sent for by an uncle, was treated en route to California. Put on a train in New York, she sat in a railroad car for almost five days without food. She was ignorant about American ways, and uncaring railroad personnel paid no attention to her. When she was met in Sacramento, she fainted from fatigue and hunger. Other naive souls ended up in towns whose names they never did learn, and where, not understanding oral directions concerning changes in trains, they spent days or nights in some local station. Another immigrant girl who did not speak English recalled how she got mixed up in her directions: "Those darn fools on the train, they put me off at the wrong station again before I got to Coalville. I didn't have anything to eat for almost two days. . . . No clothes, no money, no nothing. I can never forget."

After the first metal discoveries in Colorado in 1859, English, Welsh, Cornish and Italian hardrock miners converged there. In 1877 silver and lead discoveries at Leadville caused the sound of pick and shovel to be heard everywhere. By 1891, gold was discovered at Cripple Creek. Wielding hammers and drills, inexperienced Italian laborers came into serious economic competition with miners who had arrived earlier.

Italians bitterly remonstrated against unsatisfactory working conditions in mines, smelters, and along railroad lines. They detested the notion that they were the chattel of mine or mill owners, dependent upon them for jobs, homes, food, and education. Having fled the feudalism of the past, they did not gracefully tolerate discrimination, and 500 discontented immigrant laborers of all nationalities congregated at Denver in 1882 to protest the mine operators' broken promises. The city's Italian Consul complained to the Denver *Republican* on April 20, 1882, about the same issue. Prolonged disputes led to the formation of the Italian Protective and Benevolent Association. Soon thereafter, Italians organized a similar *Circolo Italiano.*

Labor unrest continued for years in Colorado. A tragic altercation resulted on April 20, 1914. In a tent colony established at the mining camp of Ludlow, the Italians participated in a heated demonstration over wages, hours, and working conditions. A pitched battle with mine operators followed. To quell the outbreak, state troopers raked strikers with machine gun fire and levelled the entire tent camp. Two Italian women and 13 children were burned to death. President Wilson interceded and ended the Ludlow strike. The state of Colorado paid damages for the incident, thereby accepting partial responsibility for the deaths.

The industrial strife which some immigrants encountered was offset by gratifying opportunities for employment in other Rocky Mountain areas. Marble, Colorado, became a center of quarrying operations after the turn of the century. There, Italian artisans, like those at Barre, Vermont, polished white stone by hand. At Marble, in fact, they cut the largest block of marble ever quarried—100 tons in weight; it now occupies an honored place in the nation's capital as the Tomb of the Unknown Soldier.

In 1910 the Italian-born population of Colorado reached 15,000; in the second generation, they numbered 40,000—enough persons to support various newspapers, among them *La Stella, La Nazione, Il Risveglio, La Capitale, Il Roma,* and *La Frusta* at Denver and *L'Unione* at Pueblo.

Italians named parts of this rocky land and established some of their holidays. Italian Peak (sometimes called Italia Mountain) stands at the head of the Gunnison River; Como, a town occupied after 1879, was the home of Italian coal miners. In 1907 the Italians encouraged the state legislature to make Columbus Day a legal holiday. Annually, Denver's Italians celebrate the feast of San Rocco, which commemorates the life of a priest who begged money from the rich to help the sick.

New York's *L'Eco d'Italia* encouraged Italians to push on to the Pacific Northwest. It described the abundant water, orchards, and forests that stood in such contrast to the crowded cities. The newspaper pointed out that one could find employment in sawmills, fish canneries, and logging camps and on smaller farms than in the Midwest. Although Italian Jesuits had worked with the Indians in Washington, Idaho, and Oregon, a major foreign migration did not occur until the late nineteenth century. In the 1880s, newly opened railroad lines quadrupled Washington's total population. Washington achieved statehood in 1889; after that, its magnificent lumbering country on both sides of the Cascades attracted Italians, as did the ship building and fishing industries along the deep inlets of Puget Sound.

In central Oregon a highway marker announces the location of Garibaldi to the motorist. This community of several thousand persons lies some 50 miles from Portland. According to one story, it was founded by an Italian seaman who jumped ship and remained behind to name a town after the great Giuseppe Garibaldi. His name also marks Garibaldi National Park in British Columbia.

Texas also attracted Italians, usually from the deep South. In Bryan, 2400 Sicilians who had worked as section hands on the Houston and Texas Railroad established a colony. In the 1880s, these immigrants bought bottom land at a low price because the remote area was regularly flooded. The Italians were promised free land if they would clear it of brush and timber. They sold the wood at a profit, and planted corn, cotton, and other crops. By 1900, Bryan included 500 Italian families, some of whom owned as much as 400 acres of farmland.

Although the Texas climate was sometimes uncomfortably hot, Italians were better suited to this than other foreigners were. Surprisingly, New York's *Eco d'Italia* considered Texas "the state best suited for Italians." By 1900 there was a *Società di Colonizzazione Italiana del Texas* which bought over 25,000 acres of land at Perla and Keechie. This land was divided into 50-acre lots which the organization allocated to immigrant families. It spent almost a million dollars acquiring land, farm machinery, and building materials.

The Texas Italians lived in what might be called ethnic islands, specializing in the production of staples: In southeastern Texas they grew rice; at Bryan immigrants raised corn and cotton; near Dickinson they truck-farmed berries and vegetables; at Houston and San Antonio they grew fruit; near Gunnison they raised grapes. There was more truck farming on the outskirts of Galveston and Dallas. Except for a small colony in Montague, Italians were not attracted to northern Texas, where water was scarce.

Farther into the Southwest, the population grew surprisingly cosmopolitan. The number of first-generation Italians in New Mexico nearly doubled between 1890 and 1900 after construction of the

Southern railroad. Out of Arizona came a future mayor of New York City, Fiorello La Guardia. His boyhood in remote Prescott made a lasting impression on him. Nevada also attracted scores of foreigners. In 1876 a Eureka newspaper reported that three-fourths of the migrants coming into the area were Italian charcoal burners, who made charcoal to heat the kilns. But the ten dollars they received per week was less than half that paid to other mine workers, so these burners tried to unite and strike. In 1879 a confrontation took place at Fish Creek, where several Italians were killed. The burners did not again challenge the establishment. Louis Monaco, who emigrated from Italy to Nevada, wrote letters in the local newspaper, signing his name "Veritas," pleading with mine owners:

. . . be at least humane in time to come. And since you have been made rich by these poor workers, don't raise prejudices or talk of sending an army with guns. . . . But it better becomes your duty to send an army of cheese and macaroni to quench the hunger of these poor . . . wretches who are really more hungry than ill-disposed.

An Italian–Swiss farmer in Nevada's Carson Valley recalled the discrimination he also felt during his early days: "I had to prove myself not once, but many times. I was treated worse than Negroes in the South, not by American families, but by immigrants and the sons of immigrants. . . . A schoolteacher even told my children that the Germans and British made the best citizens."

The California Gold Rush attracted many foreigners. By 1870, nearly two-thirds of its migrants were foreigners. After the turn of the century, the majority of these people settled in or around San Francisco. In 1920, Italians comprised 11.7 percent of California's foreign population—the largest foreign stock in the state.

California's mild climate and strong visual resemblance to Italy helped make Italians feel at home. Interior settlements like Asti and Lodi were named after towns in Italy. Their wines also resembled those of Italy, and the grape harvest recalled festivities in the old country. Italians cultivated patches of *basilico* (basil) to put in their *pasta* or *minestra,* and played *boccie* in the evenings.

From the 1880s onward, North Italians from Genoa, Turin, and Lombardy began to appear in California's vineyards. In 1881, banker Andrea Sbarboro interested immigrants in settling cooperatively at Asti, which he hoped would become a semi-Utopian colony. With Pietro C. Rossi as head winemaker, the Italian–Swiss agricultural colony was founded on 5000 acres of land. In 1897 its vintage was so large that there was not enough barrel cooperage in all California to hold it. Sbarboro built a cement reservoir which became the largest wine tank in the world, holding 500,000 gallons. In May 1898, when the tank was first emptied, a dance was held inside it for 200 persons. There was no crowding even though an orchestra occupied the center of the novel ballroom. The colony also had its own general store, school house, bakery, smithy, cooperage, post office, telephone and telegraph outlet, and railroad depot. The colony shipped wine eastward in railroad tank-cars and came to control much of the United States wine market.

To California's viticulture the Italians applied old-world care and new-world production methods. In 1886, Guido Rossati of the Italian Ministry of Agriculture advised local winemakers to emphasize quality over quantity. Italy's techniques of winemaking became California's, although today the industry is increasingly mechanized.

Near Los Angeles in the 1880s, Secondo Guasti's peasant tenacity led him to establish what came to be called "the globe's largest vineyard," the Italian Vineyard Company. Guasti, a Piedmontese, arrived in the United States in 1881 at the age of 21. In the semi-arid sands of Cucamonga, where other vintners refused to invest capital, Guasti planted grapes on thousands of acres. From these he produced millions of gallons of dessert wine, high in sugar as well as alcoholic content. His successors remain among the largest producers in the United States of such fortified wines as sherry, port, and angelica. Other smaller wineries eventually took over the vines he had planted. Later, in California's Central Valley, the Petri, Cribari, and Gallo families continued to meet the demand for bulk wines.

Other Italians prospered by producing high-quality wines. In the Napa Valley, the Mondavi family operates the Charles Krug Company. At Sonoma, Samuele Sebastiani began his notable winery in 1896. Later, Louis M. Martini at Saint Helena distinguished himself because of his meticulousness and quiet resolve in producing Cabernet Sauvignon and Pinot Noir grapes, which have a low yield but develop into a wine of exceptional flavor.

Not all of California's Italian agriculturists were winemakers. Beginning in 1870, many Swiss–Italians went into dairying, buying rich meadowlands from Santa Barbara north along California's coast. They built a network of farm roads from their barns to coastal wharves at San Simeon, Cambria, Cayucos, and Morro Bay. Ticinese butter- and cheese-makers clustered throughout the coast ranges, the largest number around San Luis Obispo.

Early hucksters and land speculators used the theme of California's similarity to Italy to lure new residents there. In the 1890s, the Southern Pacific Railroad Company encouraged the creation of a full-blown Mediterranean America out West. Towns named Arcadia, Tarragona, Terracina, Verona, and Venice were supposed to evoke memories of the classical ancient world. Despite the artificiality of this ballyhoo, much remains that is, in fact, Arcadian. And immigrants have played a part in refining part of North America into a Mediterranean-like area. Italian stonemasons, ironmongers, landscapers, and tile makers all enhanced the beauty of private estates, college campuses, and municipal buildings in the Golden State. California represents a high-water mark of Italian achievement in North America, much as Argentina does in the southern hemisphere.

Chapter Nine Bibliography

These books deal with Italians in outlying areas of the United States: Edmondo Mayor des Planches, *Attraverso gli Stati Uniti per l'emigrazione Italiana* (Turin, 1913); United States Immigration Commission, "Agricultural Distribution of Immigrants," in *Reports of the Immigration Commission*, 41 vols. (Washington, 1900–1911), which includes the largest collection of source materials ever assembled on all facets of immigration to the United States. Unfortunately, an index was never published. These volumes are not only invaluable, but our national restrictive quotas derived from them. See also the already mentioned volumes by Rolle, Iorizzo and Mondello, and Tomasi.

For further research on Sunnyside, see Emily Fogg Meade, "Italian Immigration into the South," *South Atlantic Quarterly*, 4 (July 1905), 217–223, and Giovanni Preziosi, *Gli Italiani negli Stati Uniti del Nord* (Milan, 1909). About Tontitown, see "Settlers in Tontitown," *Interpreter*, 8 (January 1929), 56–58, and Anita Moore, "Safe Ways To Get on the Soil: The Work of Father Bandini at Tontitown," *World's Work*, 24 (June 1912), 215–219.

Italians in Milwaukee are discussed in G. La Piana, *The Italians in Milwaukee, Wisconsin* (reprinted in San Francisco, 1970), and in Colorado in Giovanni Perilli, *Colorado and the Italians in Colorado* (Denver, 1922), and Antonia Pola, *Who Can Buy the Stars?* (New York, 1957). Foreigners in Nevada are discussed in Wilbur S. Shepperson, *Restless Strangers* (Reno, 1970). For Italians in California see Idwal Jones, *Vines in the Sun* (New York,

1949); Paul Radin, *The Italians of San Francisco* (San Francisco, 1935); Angelo Pellegrini, *Americans by Choice* (New York, 1956); Edmondo Mayor des Planches, *Gli Italiani in California* (Rome, 1904); Andrea Sbarboro, "Wines and Vineyards of California," *Overland Monthly*, 25 (January 1900), 65–79, 95–96; Vincent P. Carosso, *The California Wine Industry* (Berkeley, 1951); Mario J. Spinello, "Italians of California," *Sunset*, 14 (1904–1905), 256–258; *The Italian Theatre in San Francisco* (San Francisco, 1939), and Andrew F. Rolle, "Italy in California," *Pacific Spectator*, 9 (Autumn 1955), 408–419.

Chapter Ten

Political and Economic Achievements

While few of the earliest immigrants expected to rise to great heights economically or educationally, the shrewdest of them saw that their foremen or employers had once been workers like themselves. A poor boy could succeed in America and, in contrast to life in Italy, social and economic mobility did exist; was political mobility also available to immigrants?

In politics as in religious life in America, the Italians competed with the Irish. For example, Irish leader John Powers was boss of Chicago's nineteenth ward from 1896 to 1921. Neither the Italians nor any other ethnic group could oust him. Various anti-corruption groups sided with Jane Addams's Hull House in attempts to repudiate Powers. The city's Italian newspaper, *L'Italia*, urged Italians to work for his defeat. Yet, for years Powers boasted that he could "buy the Italian vote with a glass of beer and a compliment."

Occasionally a respected *padrone* became politically influential, perhaps by changing his name and image. Thomas Marnell, an Italian leader in Syracuse, New York, struggled for such power, not only for himself but for his constituents. He eventually was able to deliver the Italian vote in his area, a sizable achievement. Before the turn of the century, Italians in most urban areas usually voted for the Democratic Party, as did the Poles, Czechs, Germans, and Swedes.

By the late 1920s, disaffected ethnic groups changed their voting pattern and placed their faith in the Republicans. When the Great Depression hit the country, however, the Democrats forged a new, partly ethnic, consensus coalition. Among the issues that led to this political realignment were immigration restriction, the inanities of prohibition, organized crime, and ethnic as well as religious bigotry by self-righteous apologists for the old order. In New York, Alfred E. Smith's presidential campaign attracted immigrant voters; the process of political realignment was further continued by Democrat Anton Cermak's victory in Chicago's 1931 mayoralty race. He ran against a nativist who considered minority groups as not quite American. But, after Cermak's election, Chicago came to be called "the house of all peoples."

Despite discrimination, a limited number of Italians slowly entered the strange world of politics. These leaders varied widely in political philosophy. As we will see, there was a great difference between the views of Anthony Caminetti, President Wilson's Commissioner of Immigration, and those of Vito Marcantonio. Only after the 1930s could Fiorello La Guardia utilize ethnicity to gain votes. Contrary to the pressures of assimilation, the Italians have often voted as a bloc but not reliably so. Today, San Francisco's Mayor Alioto and Rhode Island's Senator Pastore are in office because of their appeal to wider audiences; in a sense, their records exemplify the emerging defeat of bigotry.

One of the first Italian–Americans to reach the national level of government was Anthony Caminetti. His father had come West during the California Gold Rush, turning later to farming. Anthony obtained a law degree at the University of California and later won seats in both the state assembly and senate. Next he was elected to the United States House of Representatives. Caminetti paradoxically championed strict immigration control. His subsequent appointment as Commissioner of Immigration in 1913 met President Wilson's need to placate immigrant public opinion as well as to represent the Far West in the cabinet. During the nativist era that followed World War I, Commissioner Caminetti clamped down on immigrants. Caminetti was an Italian who, though he never renounced his background, was totally at variance with the spirit of nonrestrictive immigration which had allowed his own parents to come to America.

Fiorello La Guardia was the first Italian–American who rose to political power without denying either his Italian or Jewish background and tastes. An extraordinary, almost apolitical figure, he became a three-term mayor of New York City. As we have seen, La Guardia had grown up in Arizona. His father, an army bandmaster, had originally come to America as an accompanist to the opera diva

Adelina Patti. Fiorello's playground had been the great outdoors where he hunted, rode, "Saw what Indians looked like, spoke to miners and cowboys, went camping in the hills with soldiers, tended the chickens and cow that his father kept, and enjoyed his share of schoolboy pranks and fights." He attributed some of his most individualistic, reformist characteristics to the almost ideal boyhood he had spent.

La Guardia's father, the leader of the 11th U.S. Infantry Band, was a popular figure who included his children in concerts. Fiorello blew the cornet while his sister played the violin and their father accompanied them on the piano. Although there was a rigid distinction between officers and enlisted men which extended to their families, this did not bother Fiorello. "I would just as soon fight an officer's kid as I would anyone else." As he recalled: "What I saw and heard and learned in my boyhood days in Arizona made lasting impressions on me. . . . For instance, I loathe the professional politician. . . . This attitude had its origin in the badly dressed, slick and sly Indian agents, political appointees, I saw come into Arizona . . . robbing the Indians of the food the government provided for them." La Guardia also remembered being ashamed of eating apples and cookies in front of hungry Indian children. In later life he was to do something about the welfare of other needy children.

"Another early impression that made its mark on my mind," La Guardia stated, "was gained from watching the railroad being built between Ashfork, Prescott, and Phoenix." Little machinery was employed during this particular construction job: "It was all manpower and draft animals. The laborers were all Mexicans and Italians." Even then he was shocked by the fact that there were no social security laws, employer liability regulations, or workmen's compensation provisions to protect immigrants or nonimmigrants. Later such memories spurred him on to fight for social equality. As he put the matter: "It was nearly half a lifetime later, as a member of Congress, that I had an opportunity of taking part in preparing the Railways Labor Act and in passage of the Norris–LaGuardia Anti-Injunction Act." Both acts were designed to protect laborers.

A final amusing, yet poignant, memory was to have its effect when La Guardia assumed power in New York. This concerned an organ grinder who came to town when he was a boy in Prescott:

He, and particularly the monkey, attracted a great deal of attention. I can hear the cries of the kids: "Dago with a monkey! Hey, Fiorello, you're a dago, too. Where's your monkey?" It hurt. And what made it worse, along came Dad, and he started to chatter in Neapolitan with the organ grinder. He hadn't spoken Italian in many years, and he seemed to enjoy it. Perhaps, too, he considered the organ grinder a fellow musician. At any rate, he promptly invited him to our house for a macaroni dinner. The kids taunted me for a long time after that. I couldn't understand it. What difference was there between us? Some of their families hadn't been in the country any longer than mine.[1]

While Mayor of New York, the Police Department informed La Guardia that roaming organ-grinders posed both a traffic menace and a hazard to small children, who rushed out onto the city streets in pursuit of them. Despite the criticism he received, the mayor banned all organ grinders from New York's public streets. He claimed that "the advent of the phonograph and the radio" as well as "free public concerts in parks, libraries, museums and other public places" made organ grinders and their monkeys obsolete. But perhaps his motive was based on the humiliation and ridicule which he had experienced on the frontier when he was likened to an illiterate, begging organ grinder.

In 1933, La Guardia was elected mayor of New York after he had served as a congressman for 14 years. He was one of the best-known political leaders of his time. He ran an efficient government and personally participated in many aspects of the city's busy life. Fiorello—or "Little Flower," as his name translated from Italian—sped to fires, went on rounds with policemen, and reported to the populace via a weekly radio program. During a newspaper strike he kept restless youngsters and adults alike informed about the latest comic strips; he read his favorite Italian recipes, as well. Immigrants found him a champion of their interests because he condemned the United States immigration quota system as bigoted. Even the Irish–Americans rallied around the mayor. He won everyone's trust, standing against government by favor and connection, which the poor once thought they needed.

Eventually other Italian–Americans served New York City. In 1950 Vincent Impellitieri became its mayor. He ran against three other contenders, all of Italian descent: Ferdinand Pecora, Edward Corsi, and Vito Marcantonio. In the background stood Carmine De

---

[1] Fiorello La Guardia, *The Making of an Insurgent* (Philadelphia, 1948), pp. 27–28.

Sapio, who had assumed control of Tammany Hall as the first Italian–American political boss with national influence. Marcantonio subsequently became the mayor's protege after La Guardia heard him give a speech at his high school. While running for Congress, Marcantonio, too, openly displayed his ethnicity. Once elected, he worked hard to defeat alien restriction legislation. During the Depression, bigots blamed the overabundance of the foreign-born for widespread unemployment, but liberals like Marcantonio repeatedly kept restriction bills from passing. In World War II, when suspicion against Italians grew, he utilized every medium to defend his countrymen. Later, Italian–Americans increasingly criticized him for his left-wing views. No one, however, worked harder for his constituents. In 1948, Italians as well as other Americans were caught up in an anti-Communist fever, and Marcantonio's support waned. In 1949 he was defeated in an election for the mayorship by Irishman William O'Dwyer. The La Guardia–Marcantonio era had come to an end.

When La Guardia was mayor of New York and Robert S. Maestri mayor of New Orleans, San Francisco also chose an Italian mayor. Angelo Rossi held that office from 1931 to 1944. Rossi was born at Volcano, California; like La Guardia, he was the son of immigrant parents. In 1967, San Francisco was to elect yet another mayor of Italian descent, prominent attorney Joseph L. Alioto, whose fisherman father had founded a restaurant on Fisherman's Wharf as well as the International Fishing Company.

The first Italian–American state governor was elected as late as 1946. John Pastore grew up in Providence, the son of an immigrant tailor. Other state governors have included New York's Charles Poletti, Washington's Albert Rosellini, and Ohio's Michael Di Salle. When Pastore became governor of Rhode Island, residents of "Little Italys" all over the country were proud of him. Whereas Italians elsewhere continued to battle politically with the Irish, Pastore did not become entangled in patronage fights with them. He awarded offices according to merit, not nationality. To do otherwise would have weakened his power, as it did that of Italian–American leaders in New York (where Carmine De Sapio's reign over Tammany Hall was toppled by the Irish). In 1950 Pastore became the first Italian–American to become a United States Senator; he is still Rhode Island's senior Senator.

In neighboring Massachusetts, John Volpe joined an increasing number of Italians in public life when he became the second Italian–American governor of that state (Foster Furcolo was governor from

1957 to 1961). Later Volpe was chosen by President Nixon to be Secretary of Transportation. He had begun his career as a hod carrier but went on to found a multimillion-dollar construction firm. In Washington the Volpes lived in Watergate, an exclusive apartment complex. One day Mrs. Volpe took her daughter to the shopping arcade on the ground floor of the complex. "Mama," she asked, "just because you come from Italy, do you still have to live above the store?"

Among Italians who have played a role in the American labor movement are Luigi Antonini and Anthony Scotto. During the 1930s, Antonini organized the Italian garment workers. Long before World War II he opposed appeasement of the Fascist regime in Italy. Because of his opposition to radicalism as well, he broke with the American Labor Party and helped to establish the tiny Liberal Party. Scotto became president of an important union within the International Longshoremen's Association, has backed civil rights, and worked for the election of the liberal mayor of New York, John Lindsay.

Ethnicity, once a powerful factor in American political life, has been receding nationally. Yet, Salvatore La Gumina has reminded us that in at least one recent election it helped to spell the defeat of a New York gubernatorial candidate, former Supreme Court Justice Arthur Goldberg. Placing his faith in a 1970 campaign pitched toward the Jewish and Negro vote, Goldberg failed to respond to the Italian–American sector to which the incumbent governor, Nelson Rockefeller, strongly appealed. Rockefeller vigorously condemned discrimination against Italian–Americans, hailed the contributions of their lodges and service clubs, and boasted about his numerous ethnic appointees to public office, promising even more of them. The result was a 35 percent shift by Italian–American voters from the Democratic Party to the Republicans.

Ethnic groups do not merely seek a candidate of their own nationality, but a candidate who is attractive and vigorous as well. An appeal on purely ethnic grounds may well end in defeat for an unattractive candidate. Yet, to slight national sensibilities may spell disaster for a candidate or a party, especially in the northeastern United States. In the western part of the country only San Francisco exhibits the same sense of loyalty toward its Italian, Irish, and Chinese leadership. San Francisco's Mayor Alioto and State Assembly Leader Robert Moretti testify to the continuing strength of Italian influence in California.

It was in the Golden State that Amadeo Pietro Giannini, the son of a Ligurian immigrant, founded the largest financial institution in the United States. Other Italian bankers, Felix Argenti and Andrea Sbarboro, preceded Giannini, but his record overshadowed them all. His bank came to be linked not only with immigrants but also with the growth of California itself. His first success came out of the activities of immigrants on the land. The price of western farms at the turn of the century was exorbitant. To equip and to operate a farm was beyond the means even of some native farmers. Refused loans by large banks, immigrants looked to local merchants for capital. These pseudo-bankers also acted as penny-pinching real-estate brokers, business advisers, and tax consultants.

Just as J. P. Morgan had been the banker for men of great wealth, Giannini became the spokesman for a later generation of small ranchers, fruit peddlers, fishermen, and ordinary workmen. He first organized the Bank of Italy to aid San Francisco's Italian colony, clustered along its North Beach. Giannini preached the advantages of interest-bearing savings accounts and announced that he would lend a worker as much as $25 "with no better security than the callouses on the borrower's hands."

The 1906 earthquake and fire paradoxically gave Giannini some special opportunities. With all other banks closed and the ashes of the fire still warm, he transacted a brisk business along the San Francisco waterfront. During the quake, Giannini had hidden cash, gold, and bank records under a wagonload of oranges. North Beach immigrants had never before trusted bankers; now, when they desperately needed cash, Giannini won their trust by allowing depositors to make small withdrawals. After the fire they brought him gold hoarded in stockings, tin boxes, and mattresses—gold which helped to rebuild San Francisco. Later, Giannini's Bank of Italy extended its operations and changed its name to the Bank of America.

Giannini was an innovator who kept an iron grip on his local branch managers, who were frequently Italians. He also allowed immigrant families to voice their wishes about how the bank should be run. In fact, Giannini's very success stemmed from his obvious interest in all aspects of a depositor's life. He once said that anything which concerned people should also interest banks. For Italian–Americans, Giannini became a symbol of success in the most respectable of all businesses. His achievement was then unusual in the American environment, requiring special insight and imagination.

One need not focus only upon well-known public figures to understand successful Italian–Americans. Paolo Sindaco, for example, advanced from a humble coal miner to a mine owner. August Scolio began as a grocery clerk and became the largest wholesaler of fruit and produce in Erie, New York. Pasquale D'Agostino operated a pushcart through the streets of New York City's East Harlem, then opened a small food store, and finally launched a larger store which still employs hundreds of people and sells millions of dollars worth of groceries each year. The first Italian–American millionaire was Generoso Pope. As a young boy he worked on a road gang; later he bought sand and gravel pits and ran a contracting business. He published *Il Progresso Italo Americano* of New York, the most widely read Italian–American newspaper in this country. His son carries on his enterprises.

Today, Americans of all backgrounds enjoy cosmopolitan foods partly because of Italian influence. Giuseppe Taormino, a Sicilian, began peddling food to Italian workers from a cart in New Orleans. From this small beginning came the well-known Progresso Company. John Taormino, who today heads the company, recalls that as immigrants prospered, their taste in food became increasingly sophisticated. The Peanut King, Amedeo Obici, came to this country with only five cents in his pocket. Eventually, he set up a fruit and vegetable stand, roasting and selling peanuts as a sideline. In 1906 he incorporated the Planter Peanut Company which has expanded throughout the world.

In California Joseph Maggio became the "Carrot King of the United States." California vintners of Italian descent—among them the Gallos, Petris, and Martinis—helped introduce Americans to wine on a national scale. Some of California's largest producers of fruit and vegetables were Italian immigrants who exported their products to eastern and later worldwide markets.

In 1889, thirty years after he arrived in the United States, Marco J. Fontana founded the California Fruit Packing Corporation. Calpac, as it is now known, became the largest fruit and vegetable canning organization in the world. In the early days of the Italian Swiss Colony, Fontana had worked at Asti for his fellow Ligurian, banker Andrea Sbarboro. Fontana originated the brand name Marca del Monte, later shortened to the popular Del Monte label. By 1965, long after Fontana's death, Calpac owned 24,000 acres of land and leased another 74,000. Today, it contracts annually for the crops of hundreds of farms and owns canneries and warehouses throughout the United States.

Joseph Di Giorgio has a similar history. By 1893 this immigrant was an importer and then a grower in the southern San Joaquin Valley. He founded the Di Giorgio Fruit Corporation with his brother, Rosario. After 1910 the Di Giorgios controlled crop-yielding land, bought the crops of other growers, and canned as well as sold produce under the S & W label. They became the largest shippers of fresh fruit in the world, managing or owning more than 40,000 acres of land in California, South America, Central America, and Mexico. Following Italian agricultural tradition, the several thousand farm workers the Di Giorgios employed lived in company towns on various ranches.

Imagination, determination, and thrift—often in place of education—brought these Italians to prominence. Close-knit families worked together to make a business succeed. The children of such entrepreneurs had better opportunities for education. As a result, they brought new ideas into the family business or entered the professions of medicine, law, or teaching.

Perhaps the political and economic figures we have introduced in this chapter were not typical of the millions of Italians who entered the country with them. The La Guardias, Gianninis, and Aliotos distinguished themselves far beyond the capabilities of their compatriots. Among the second generation, too, Lido Iacocca, who became President of the Ford Motor Company, represents atypical achievement. Yet, these are the persons whose record the historian can document. It is difficult to find statistics concerning the social mobility of immigrants, Italian or otherwise. Furthermore, we have an obligation to honor the achievements of our national groups as well as to examine their shortcomings.

Chapter Ten Bibliography

Descriptions of the careers of various Italians appear in D'Angelo, *Son of Italy;* Federal Writers' Project, *The Italians of New York;* Marinacci, *They Came from Italy;* Rolle, *The Immigrant Upraised;* Iorizzo and Mondello, *The Italian–Americans;* Pisani, *The Italian in America;* Schiavo, *Four Centuries* and his *Italian–American Who's Who* (New York, 1938). More recently, Alexander De Conde's *Half Bitter, Half Sweet* (New York, 1972) mentions selected individuals.

On La Guardia see Arthur Mann, *La Guardia, A Fighter against His Times, 1882–1933* (Philadelphia, 1959) and the mayor's own *Fiorello H. La Guardia, The Making of an Insurgent, An Autobiography, 1882–1919* (Philadelphia,

1948). For Marcantonio see Salvatore J. La Gumina, *Vito Marcantonio, The People's Politician* (Dubuque, 1969), and Alan L. Schaffer, *Vito Marcantonio, Radical in Congress* (Syracuse, 1966). An early article on Pastore is Samuel Lubell, "Rhode Island's Little Firecracker," *Saturday Evening Post,* 222 (November 12, 1949). On Carmine De Sapio, see Warren Moscow, *The Last of the Big-Time Bosses, The Life and Times of Carmine De Sapio* (New York, 1971). Recent scholarship about a key election is Salvatore J. La Gumina's "Ethnic Groups in the New York Elections of 1970," *New York History,* 53 (January 1972), 55–71.

Information about Amadeo Giannini is in the already cited books of Marinacci, Rolle, as well as Marquis and Bessie R. James, *Biography of a Bank, the Story of Bank of America* (New York, 1954). See also Dwight L. Clarke, "The Gianninis, Men of the Renaissance," *California Historical Society Quarterly,* 49 (September 1970), 251–269 and (December 1970), 337–351. On Fermi, see Marinacci as well as Laura Fermi, *Illustrious Immigrants, The Intellectual Migration from Europe, 1930–1941* (Chicago, 1968).

Chapter Eleven

The Professions, Culture, and the Spiritual Life

Reliable statistics about immigrant occupations are difficult to compile and sometimes incomplete. Italians were involved in every field. Usually classified as day laborers, large numbers of them continued to work in factories and mill towns. They formed a high proportion of those who were tailors, miners, quarrymen, railroad hands, and construction workers. In the late nineteenth century, about 10 percent of them worked as carpenters, marble carvers, stone masons, and plasterers. Others labored in logging camps, in agriculture, or as gardeners.

In 1903, the number of professionals entering the United States from Italy was still distinctly limited. The majority of Italians in 1903 came from southern Italy (see table on p. 96).

As discrimination toward them waned, immigrants gradually entered the professions. At first Italian physicians and lawyers practiced only in Italian-speaking neighborhoods. There, difficulty with the English language was not a factor for doctors, dentists, and pharmacists of Italian descent. As compared to other nationalities—for example, the Germans—Italians seemed slower to achieve professional status. Only as they gained a measure of affluence could they send their children to graduate schools of law, dentistry, and medicine. Most of the earliest Italian physicians had been trained in the old country.

An exception was Dr. Tullio Verdi, personal physician of Secretary of State William Seward and other political leaders at the capital. In 1856 he received a medical degree from Philadelphia's Hahnemann

Occupations of Italian Immigrants in 1903

	Northern Italy	Southern Italy
Professionals (engineers, lawyers, bankers, physicians, teachers, etc.)	266	551
Tradesmen (bakers, barbers, masons, painters, plumbers, etc.)	6,766	24,895
Other laborers (including farmers)	24,284	118,751

Source: Annual Report of the Commissioner of Immigration (Washington, D.C., 1903).

College. Verdi had arrived in the United States with only five dollars. After teaching Italian at Brown University, he turned to medicine and was the first native of Italy to graduate from an American medical school. Dr. Verdi's name was used by the plotters of the Lincoln assassination in order to enter Seward's home.

Italian scientists also found their way to America. Among the first to seek political asylum was Quirico Filopanti. He came to America in 1849, but returned to Italy in 1866 to fight alongside Garibaldi. Filopanti later sought funds in the United States for experiments in air navigation. Although his ideas were not considered practical at that time, New York's *Eco d'Italia* voiced its sympathy: "Columbus and Fulton also had to struggle against the prejudices of their century."

In the 1870s, after Italy's national unification, learned persons were freer to travel than before. More vessels also crossed the Atlantic with greater rapidity. In 1876 the International Centennial Exposition in Philadelphia, honoring the first hundred years of American independence, drew Italian intellectuals to the United States. The scientists among them were impressed with its prosperity, democracy, and industrialization. Some wished to pursue their studies and experiments in the new country, for, Italy, then as now, was deficient in providing laboratories and research facilities for its scholars.

Slowly, Italian technicians overcame the language and economic barriers. Among these was Giuseppe Bellanca, an aviation pioneer who came to the United States in 1911. His monoplane, the *Columbia,* was the first cabin aircraft to cross the Atlantic ocean. Bellanca also designed and built the first trans-Pacific monoplane, the *Miss Veedol.* A Bellanca two-seater is still a popular airplane manufactured in the United States.

Scientists of Italian descent helped to develop atomic energy. The most prominent of these was Enrico Fermi, the first physicist to perfect a nuclear chain reaction and the father of atomic fission. In 1930 Fermi was invited to lecture at the University of Michigan. Eight years later he won the Nobel Prize in physics. Disgusted with Mussolini, he refused to give the Fascist salute at the Nobel Prize ceremony; he had become disillusioned with conditions in Italy, where his Jewish wife had experienced racial discrimination. After Columbia University appointed him Professor of Physics in 1939, Albert Einstein wrote a letter to President Roosevelt on Fermi's discoveries. This may have changed the course of history, for Einstein warned of the implications of Germany's uranium research. Later, Roosevelt set up the Special Uranium Committee.

At the University of Chicago, Fermi constructed the first successful atomic pile, leading to a self-sustaining chain reaction which began the atomic age. After Fermi moved his research group to Los Alamos, New Mexico, the atomic bomb was first tested. After the war, Fermi hoped nuclear power would be used for peace and continued work until his death in 1954.

Professor Bruno Rossi worked with Fermi at Los Alamos but he is best known for his research on cosmic rays. Rossi was born in Venice, studied at Bologna, and taught at Florence, Padua, and Manchester before coming to the United States in 1939. He taught at the University of Chicago, Cornell, and the Massachusetts Institute of Technology. His astrophysical research, carried out for the National Aeronautics and Space Administration, contributed to the 1970 Explorer X project. This was the first of a series of astronomy satellites launched at the Italian Aerospace Centre off the coast of Kenya. In 1971, Italy's Accademia dei Lincei awarded Rossi one of its 20-million-lira ($30,000) awards.

Three Italian scientists who moved to America have won Nobel Prizes—Fermi and Emilio Segrè in physics and Salvador Luria in virology. Yet, it was relatively rare to find Italians in a number of other areas of cultural achievement. Only slowly did the Italian–Americans penetrate the educational establishment. They still remain underrepresented in the Ivy League and in America's other universities and colleges. Henry Suzzalo, President of the University of Washington from 1915 to 1926, was one of the few who became early national leaders. Suzzalo went on to be President of the Carnegie Foundation.

By the 1950s, however, Pietro Belluschi was Dean of the School of Architecture at the Massachusetts Institute of Technology. He won the 1972 gold medal of the American Institute of Architects, the highest award of the Institute. In 46 years of practice, Belluschi designed more than 1000 buildings. Among the most notable are his churches, residences that became internationally known as architecture typical of the Pacific Northwest, and the first glass-and-aluminum curtain-wall skyscraper built in the United States, the Equitable Building completed in Portland in 1948. Among his works are the Julliard School at Lincoln Center, done in association with other architects.

The Italians have been remiss about chronicling their history in this country in contrast to other ethnic groups. The *American Jewish Historical Quarterly* dates from 1892, and this journal boasts a distinguished board of editors. The *American Scandinavian Historical Review* began publication in 1912. Occasional Italian publications have been started, among them those of Columbia University's Casa Italiana. But as late as 1972, there is no regularly published Italian–American historical journal. Only in the late 1960s was the American Italian Historical Society founded, appropriately on Staten Island where so many immigrants first landed.

Novels concerning immigrant life in America, Italian or otherwise, have not attracted a large reading audience. Usually Italian–American novels are overly sentimental, featuring an outpouring of past hurts before a final personal victory. Only occasionally have these books attained the status of good literature. Italian nuns, bricklayers, grocers, and other immigrants of all ages and types have repeatedly been portrayed. Novels and autobiographies sometimes mirror ethnicity better than the writings of sociologists or historians. Second-generation writers have drawn from their own experiences and those of their parents to recreate the immigrant's problems. The number of Italo–American authors has not been great; perhaps this is because some Italian families felt that reading and writing were frivolous undertakings which detracted from material achievement. The anti-intellectualism of American life reinforced this belief.

A few years before World War II, Pietro DiDonato's *Christ in Concrete* became a best-seller. DiDonato portrayed the rude world of the construction worker in the 1920s and 1930s as revealed through the eyes of Paulie, an adolescent son of an Italian family in New York City. Paulie loses his father in a heartbreaking accident and fights his own passive resignation toward the injustices his family sustains. After entering construction work, he goes to night school and enlarges his horizons. In DiDonato's best seller, Paulie's Americanization clashes with his family's value system.

Jere Mangione's *Mount Allegro* describes life within a Sicilian family in Rochester, New York. A son travels to Sicily, feeling at home there in a mystical sense. The idea of returning to the country of one's origins is also movingly told by Jo Pagano in *The Paesanos*. Pagano drew from his own experiences in his *Golden Wedding* and *The Condemned*. Immigrant hardships are depicted by Pascal d'Angelo in *Son of Italy*. D'Angelo wrote poetry despite the drudgery of his life as a laborer. Poverty forms the background for John Fante's *Wait until Spring, Bandini* and *Dago Red*. Fante describes the immigrant's loneliness, alienation, and despair. This, of course, was not only an Italian problem but a universal one in an age when other foreigners sought identity in an Anglicized society. John Ciardi is another Italian–American poet of note, although he does not celebrate his Italian background. Angelo Pellegrini, an English professor at the University of Washington, describes six Italian–Americans in *Americans by Choice* and has written an autobiography entitled *Immigrant's Return*.

More recently, Mario Puzo's best seller, *The Godfather,* has described the demimonde of the Mafia and the role of Italian criminals. The American *Mafiosi* are not quite depicted as the reverse racists and hypocrites which they are. Gay Talese's *Honor Thy Father,* instead, shows how these criminals close their society to women who, though protected and indulged, become depersonalized captives. Talese's book is supposedly based on the life of Joe Bonanno.

Italian–Americans have become extremely sensitive about such portrayals. In 1970, the Italian–American Civil Rights League persuaded the filmmakers of Puzo's book to excise the term "Mafia" from their screen play. That same year the United States Department of Justice officially stopped using the words "Mafia" and "Cosa Nostra."

Drawing upon their heritage of excellence in art and music, Italian artists and musicians in America have been better known than novelists and poets. Non-Italian singers once used Italian names to further their careers. Enrico Caruso, no doubt, remains the best known of all singers. The Metropolitan Opera Company brought the most talented performers to New York. Along with Caruso, American audiences heard Antonio Scotti, Titta Ruffo, Giovanni Martinelli, Beniamino Gigli, Amelita Gallicurci, Vivian Della Chiesa, Licia Albanese, Marguerite Piazza, Ezio Pinza, and many others. The handsome basso Pinza left the Metropolitan to appear in stage musicals (*South Pacific* and *Fanny*) as well as in the movies. A man who came to control these artists was James Petrillo, sometimes called the "Little Caesar" of the music industry. As president of the powerful entertainment union called ASCAP, Petrillo (like the Russian impresario Sol Hurok) represented composers, instrumentalists, and conductors who traveled in America but never settled here.

Arturo Toscanini never became a citizen, but for years he conducted in America. Although Toscanini was a cellist, he stepped in for an absent conductor in 1867 while on tour in South America and continued to conduct to the end of his life, driving performers toward the perfection he sought. Stories about his meticulousness and short temper became legion. In 1898 he became the director of La Scala in Milan and gave that opera house new life. Ten years later Toscanini accepted the New York Metropolitan Opera Company's offer to conduct its orchestra. During World War I, Toscanini went back to Italy to assist in its war effort. After the Armistice, he was asked to reorganize La Scala. Although Fascism became popular, he refused to display Mussolini's portrait at La Scala. Life became so uncomfortable for Toscanini that he returned to the United States.

At Carnegie Hall the maestro's concerts were always sold out. Via radio (and television after 1948), people throughout the world listened to the New York Philharmonic Orchestra with Toscanini conducting. In 1937 the National Broadcasting Company created an orchestra for Toscanini. The RCA Victor Company recorded his concerts in a specially designed sound studio in Rockefeller Center. Toscanini worked with that orchestra for 16 years. Following World War II, Toscanini returned to Italy and conducted a concert at his beloved La Scala, rebuilt after the bombing of Milan. He eventually retired to Italy, where he died in 1957.

The best known modern Italo–American composer is Giancarlo Menotti. His opera, *Amahl and the Night Visitors,* was commissioned for television. Frank Loesser converted Sidney Howard's play, *They Knew What They Wanted* into a popular musical entitled *The Most Happy Fella,* set in California's Italianate Napa Valley vineyards. Choral works, sacred music, symphonic poems, instrumental pieces, and popular music like that of Henry Mancini, have also come from Americans of Italian descent. Russ Colombo and Guy Lombardo became well-known bandleaders. Popular Italo–American vocalists include Frank Sinatra, Perry Como, Vic Damone, and Dean Martin. Some of their children have continued in the entertainment field.

From the nineteenth century onward, several well known Italian actors and actresses appeared in America but gave their performances in Italian. Adelaide Ristori was supported by an Italian-speaking cast at her first appearance and only later by English-speaking actors. Eleonora Duse also performed in Italian.

The most romantic name in the history of Hollywood is still that of Rudolph Valentino. Frank Capra won several Academy Awards for directing such films as *Wild Is the Wind,* in which Anna Magnani and Anthony Quinn portrayed the conflicts posed by an emotional Italian wife brought to a western sheep ranch. Academy Award winner Anne Bancroft was born Anna Italiano. Jimmy Durante was a vaudeville performer, then a radio comedian, and later a movie and television comic.

In the visual arts, Italians worked in many media. Monuments and statues were executed by the Piccirilli family; Attilio, a native of Massa Carrara came to the United States with his brothers and guided them in producing massive marble works. In 1921, Simon Rodia (Rodilla) started to build some bizarre towers in Watts, a suburb of Los Angeles. He fashioned these out of bits of glass, tile, and pieces of junk. Because he had no building permit, Rodia had many disputes with city officials over safety as he erected other taller and odder structures. Everyone thought he was crazy as they saw him working on the towers, fastened with a window-washer's belt and singing Italian arias. Constant bickering about the towers' safety embittered Rodia and he stopped building them. In the 1950s, after a government test of their strength, Rodia's towers were declared a monument to be protected by the Los Angeles Cultural Heritage Board.

In almost every American city, Italian workmen—stonemasons, terrazo-layers, and landscapers—have created parks which attest to their skills. Roman-born Beniamino Bufano created unique sculpture for San Francisco. One statue, "Peace," stands at the entrance to the International Airport, and his "Saint Francis" overlooks the city's waterfront.

Less well known are Joseph Stella's sketches, which caught the apprehensive mood of foreigners about to start their new life as they left Ellis Island. They remind one of Jacob Epstein's early pen-and-ink drawings. Both artists aided reformers by depicting social and economic injustices. Stella's later studies concentrated on participation of the foreign-born in industry. Some of his best drawings portrayed the interplay of muscle power and impersonal machines in the steel mills of the new world.

More recently Ted Ettore De Grazia has become a well known Southwestern artist. His *Los Ninos* was used as one of UNICEF's 1964 Christmas cards. De Grazia utilizes the barren Southwestern landscape to highlight drawings of Indians, horses, and children of all races. Another Southwesterner, Paolo Soleri, designs cities of the future. A California illustrator and author, Leo Politi, has delighted children and adults alike with his colorful books. In *Little Leo* he describes his childhood visit to Italy. Wearing an Indian outfit, he became the idol of a small Italian village and picked up an Italian accent!

No description of immigrant life in America would be complete without a discussion of the role of religion in immigrants' lives. We have noted the activities of early missionaries from Italy and parish churches established for Italian immigrants by the 1860s.

The Italian attitude toward religion has historically been ambivalent. While women were bound to the mass, the sacraments, and confession, Italian men frequently hated the clergy and its control over family morals. Men rarely went to mass. Despite devotion to particular saints and the celebration of special feast days, the majority of immigrants were poorly instructed in religious matters.

Antipapal propaganda among political exiles devoted to unification of Italy (which the church opposed) was strong even after the *Risorgimento* struggle ended. Educated Italians in the New World regarded themselves as "cultural Catholics" but felt that the papacy was the enemy of liberty and progress. Furthermore, the Italo–American press had championed the cause of a united Italy at the expense of a united church. At a time when local priests censured Garibaldi from their pulpits, Chicago's Italians wanted to name a school in his honor.

At first the Italians were grouped within Irish congregations, sometimes forced to meet in church basements. Some Irish, resenting the intrusion of so many Italians, moved out of these parishes or made Italians feel ashamed and uneasy about their imagistic public processions as well as their inability to understand announcements in the English language. The anticlericalism of Italian parishioners scandalized the Irish prelates who oversaw their religious life.

Italian parishioners were sometimes niggardly in support of these churches. In the old country, religion had been sustained by government aid. No tradition of local support existed. Irish, German, and Polish Catholics were usually more loyal to their parishes than the

Italians. Not only did rivalries occur between these nationalities; Italians were also torn by regional jealousies of Tuscans, Neapolitans, Genoese, or Calabrians. They were even divided over their faith. The folk beliefs of South Italian hill people included sorcery and single-minded veneration of relatively unknown local saints. This approach to religion was unacceptable to sophisticated city dwellers, especially the North Italians. Although relatively rare, clerical greed and the immorality of a few priests, whether Irish or Italian, further set back the cause of a united immigrant loyalty to religion.

By the 1880s, both the Vatican and the American Catholic clergy were concerned that immigrants might defect from Catholicism due to traditional anticlerical biases imported from the homeland and reinforced by socialist dogma. Mass immigration of millions of Italians to urban settings increased these fears. The Americanization centers set up by several denominations posed a threat, although only a small fraction of Catholics became Protestants. Suspicious of Baptists, Methodists, and other denominations, most resisted evangelization.

Yet, only an occasional *festa* seemed to bind together those Catholic Italians who continued to attend mass in the basements of Irish and German parishes while their non-Italian mortgage holders prayed upstairs. Whenever superstitious "wops" spoke of warding off the evil spirit (*Il malocchio*), they were subjected to further derision. Educated clergymen looked down upon illiterate charges and sometimes actually regarded their village mentalities as so foreign that priests felt more comfortable with non-Italian parishioners. Conversely, many emigrants from southern Italy hated being placed under the tutelage of seemingly cold and emotionally distant northern Italians. As for American onlookers, they saw that some Italians incorporated paganism, superstition, and ritual into their worship and were mystified. But the most rustic of these fundamentalists frequently offered the strongest opposition to being evangelically converted by America's Protestant faiths.

The Italians in almost every major city from Boston to Los Angeles, however, continued to support ethnic parishes. These were churches in which the native language continued to be used and where traditional services were held. Parish schools also taught children the Italian language and the customs of the old homeland. The ethnic churches provided socially isolated immigrants with a continuing national context. However, they did not unify the Italian communities even though they long operated successful parochial schools, convents, and hospitals. Mostly the ethnic parishes filled an important gap during a crucial period of assimilation into American life because their priests maintained the familiar patterns of the homeland. South Italian immigrants, in particular, embellished their prayers with statues of local saints, special feast days, and ornate celebrations. Some immigrant communities held more than 30 religious celebrations per year. As late as the 1960s there were 74 Italian churches in New York alone.

In 1887, Bishop Scalabrini of Piacenza founded the Congregation of the Missionaries of Saint Charles in order to operate Italian churches across the United States. Nine years later, Salesian priests landed at San Francisco to serve the Italians there. The Franciscan order also increased its missionary efforts in the large cities as the new century approached.

The most revered Italian religious leader in America was Mother Francesca Xavier Cabrini, founder of the Order of the Missionary Sisters of the Sacred Heart and the first American citizen elevated to sainthood. Mother Cabrini started a missionary order for nuns and opened schools, convents, orphanages, and training centers in Italy. At Rome, Bishop Scalabrini convinced Mother Cabrini that she could bridge the gulf between the old and the new culture among the Italian poor in the United States. In 1889 Mother Cabrini arrived in New York with six nuns. When she met Irish Archbishop Corrigan, he told her that the orphanage to which she had been assigned was nonexistent and suggested that her group return to Italy. But, witnessing Mother Cabrini's determination, he arranged for her nuns to teach Italian children at St. Joachin's Church near Mulberry Street.

From this small beginning, Mother Cabrini and her order established orphanages, schools, and finally hospitals in New York. The Archbishop of New Orleans asked her to start a mission there. She bought a tenement house and converted it into a convent, and she founded a center for Italian social life, a school, and an orphanage. The New Orleans pattern was followed in other American cities and in Latin America.

By 1906, on the twenty-fifth anniversary of the founding of her order, Mother Cabrini had missions in eight countries, operated by a thousand sisters, most of whom she had recruited in Italy. A tireless worker, she died in Chicago in 1917. After her death, miracles and cures were attributed to her and, in 1946, Pope Pius XII canonized Mother Cabrini as "Saint of the Immigrants."

Italian immigrants resented continued monopolization of the United States Catholic hierarchy by the Irish–American clergy.

Whereas earlier bishops (among them Rosati) had been Italian or had reflected Italian tastes, as late as 1950 not one bishop (of the more than 100 in the United States) was of Italian origin. America's Irish community amassed wealth earlier than the Italians, which helped them to dominate the church hierarchy, however unfair the situation seemed to other immigrant groups.

Foreign Catholics in America (and particularly the Italians in whose country the Vatican is located) felt themselves to be under Irish control. Yet bishops are not created by Rome but are appointed upon recommendation of the national hierarchies. These, in turn, were influenced by their strongly Irish parishes, from which they derived their financial support. Although the Italians remained communicants, they were not a majority force within their own church. While leaders of Italian descent advanced in other fields, they were blocked inside the American Catholic hierarchy. The result was that, by 1972 some 57 percent of its bishops were of Irish extraction while only 17 percent of American Catholics were Irish. That year there were only nine bishops of Italian background in the United States, even though more than half of an estimated 21 million American Italians remained active Catholics. In California, which contained almost 400,000 persons of Italian descent in 1972, there was only one bishop with an Italian surname. Other important American states have no bishops of Italian, or even Latin, descent.

In 1971 Monsignor Geno Baroni, head of the National Center for Urban Ethnic Affairs, said: "Someday, some Italian–American priest is going to write a book about Mother Church, and it's going to make *Portnoy's Complaint* look like nothing." The church, he avers, taught immigrants "how to be Americans by running away from our cultural heritage, our accents, our languages, our food." Baroni reflects a strong Italo–American feeling that the church can now draw strength from its cosmopolitan past by fostering ethnic diversity.

While religion was once undeniably essential to many of the earliest immigrants, as time went on it no longer had the same meaning for their children. Other aspects of American life seemed to replace veneration of spiritual values. The materialism of American society, its consumer-oriented advertising and production system, and a hundred distractions took the younger generation toward other interests. Sports, for example, fascinated most immigrant children. The central position of athletics in the American system—in terms of conferring acceptability, glamour, and wealth upon the successful—made it almost a national religion. Boxing and baseball attracted countless young Italian boys who aspired to match the achievements of Primo Carnera, Rocky Marciano, Rocky Graziano, Tony Lazzeri, Joe Di-Maggio, Phil Rizzuto, and Yogi Berra.

The Horatio Alger image in a modified form—to be even more successful than other Americans—had become the goal of many immigrants. On Columbus Day, immigrant newspapers and speeches at meetings of lodges and fraternal organizations extolled Italian achievements in all fields. After so much struggle, a measure of self-congratulation was understandable.

Chapter Eleven Bibliography

Analyses of the relationship between the Catholic Church and the Italians are to be found in Tomasi and Engel, pp. 163–213, and in Rudolph J. Vecoli, "Prelates and Peasants," *Journal of Social History,* 2 (Spring 1969), 217–268. On continuing frictions, consult "Has the Church Lost Its Soul?" *Newsweek,* October 4, 1971, 80–89. Mother Cabrini's life has inspired several authors, among them Marinacci, pp. 95–114, Pietro DiDonato in his *Immigrant Saint —The Life of Mother Cabrini* (New York, 1960), and Theodore Maynard, *Too Small a World; The Life of Francesca Cabrini* (Milwaukee, 1945). Toscanini is sympathetically treated in Marinacci, pp. 115–135. An inspiring story by an educator, Leonard Covello, is *The Heart Is the Teacher* (New York, 1958). A book on the artist Stella is by Irma B. Jaffe, *Joseph Stella* (Cambridge, 1970).

Representative novels by Italians are Valenti Angelo, *The Golden Gate* (New York, 1939); Michael De Capite, *No Bright Banner* (New York, 1944); Pietro DiDonato, *Christ in Concrete* (New York, 1939) and *Three Circles of Light* (New York, 1960); John Fante, *Dago Red* (New York, 1940) and *Wait until Spring, Bandini* (New York, 1938); Jerre Mangione, *Mount Allegro* (New York, 1942); Jo Pagano, *The Condemned* (New York, 1947), *Golden Wedding* (New York, 1943), and *The Paesanos* (New York, 1940); Leo Politi, *Little Leo* (New York, 1951); and Antonia Pola, *Who Can Buy the Stars?* (New York, 1957).

Olga Peragallo is editor of *Italian–American Authors and Their Contribution to American Literature* (New York, 1949). Recent novels dealing with the Italo–American theme are: Lucas Longo, *The Family on Vendetta Street* (New York, 1968); Jerre Mangione, *America Is Also Italian* (New York, 1969), and *Passion for Sicilians: The World around Danilo Dolci* (New York, 1970); Joe Vergara, *Love and Pasta* (New York, 1968); Ralph Corsel, *Up There the Stars* (New York, 1968); Joseph Arleo, *The Grand Street Collector* (New York,

1970); and Mario Puzo, *The Godfather* (New York, 1969). A book of readings, including selections by Gino Speranza, Rocco Corresca, and Antonio Mangano, is Appel, *New Immigration*. See also Glanz's sensitive and warm comparative study, *Italian and Jew*.

Chapter Twelve

Beyond Adjustment

Prejudice against newcomers in America waxed and waned. In times of prosperity and economic expansion, antiforeignism receded. But it grew during the last troublesome decades of the nineteenth century, when southern European immigrants were blamed for unemployment, labor upheavals, and slums. Nativists and labor leaders believed that foreign workers would lower the national standard of living. Popular journals advocated literacy tests to keep them out of the country. Anti-Catholic newspapers warned of the mysterious control that rabbis and priests allegedly held over immigrants. While intellectuals may have admired the Italians' Mediterranean culture, the peasant immigrants were difficult to relate to the heritage of Rome. Many people saw them as a corruptive influence.

After Italy fought with the Allies in World War I, anti-Italian feeling was temporarily reduced. Unassimilated citizens were suddenly inducted into the army, and immigrants seemed to be more welcome in the mainstream of American life. As Pietro DiDonato had one of his characters say in his *Three Circles of Light:* "Then I was not a dago wop kid, but an American boy."

After the war, hostility toward hyphenated Americans reappeared. During the 1920s, some of them joined the extreme reform wing of the labor movement which was threatening to the establishment. A few were accused of being anarchists. A class-conscious cult of white Anglo-Saxonism swept the country. One of its results was the 1924 Quota System Act which reinforced the myth of Nordic racial supremacy. During those bitter years Nicola Sacco and Bartolomeo Vanzetti were accused of robbing and then killing a paymaster and guard at a shoe factory in South Braintree, Massachusetts. Puritan

New England came to view these admitted radicals and anarchists as alien agitators. During their trial American Catholics, conversely, saw them as untouchable apostates. Despite the subsequent confession of a prison inmate that he had committed the murders, the Massachusetts Supreme Court refused to upset the guilty verdict against the two Italians. Because of criticism of the decision, Massachusetts' governor appointed a committee to review the trial record; the committee deemed the conviction just. Numerous intellectuals, among them Albert Einstein, George Bernard Shaw, John Dos Passos, and Felix Frankfurter, protested the verdict. Edna Saint Vincent Millay based her poem "Wine from These Grapes" upon the plight of Sacco and Vanzetti while the Jewish artist Ben Shahn, created a moving painting in their memory. They were executed on August 23, 1927, in spite of repeated attempts to save their lives. Were Sacco and Vanzetti framed by self-righteous bigots? About his plight Vanzetti humbly stated: "If it had not been for these things I might have live out my life talking at street corners to scorning men, I might have die unmarked, unknown, a failure. Now we are not a failure. This is our career and our triumph. Never in our full life could we hope to do such work for tolerance, for joostice, for man's understanding of man as now we do by accident. Our words—our lives—our pains—nothing! The taking of our lives— lives of a good shoemaker and a fish-peddler—all! That last moment belongs to us—that agony is our triumph."

Although nativism has not been unique to the United States, it has caused bitterness and distrust. Americans tended to look favorably upon foreigners who had "adjusted," or become "our kind of people," but Italians retained differences in their names, language, or darker skin tone. Even the odors of garlic and *Toscano* cigars made them stand out. When the "best" values were presented as Anglo or American, foreigners felt the need to hide old identities and habits to succeed in the new country; few rebelled against American values. Yet, immigrants were adjusting to a relatively adolescent culture since the United States was still attempting to define its own style. Intolerant of variety whenever violence broke out, newspapers stressed nationality. Even trivial altercations in the Italian ghettoes caused headlines.

The peer-oriented Italians followed a social pattern that resisted change and sometimes even nobility. Self-conscious and ill at ease about entering middle-class life, they reacted with humility on the one hand as well as by dramatic overstatement when faced with imagined or genuine discrimination against them. The Italians particularly seemed to need acceptance. Whereas Germans sometimes settled in closed communities and fought to maintain their native language and culture, the Italians were rarely *chiusi,* or closed, critical, and superior in attitude. Most felt bound to adopt American values at least until they had achieved more than marginal success. Then they could return to their own ways either in America or in Italy. Their assimilation, however, was often so complete that it was impossible to return to the old style of life.

Abandoning old ways was disheartening, yet it was important to learn the new language. When a newly-arrived countryman spoke Italian, it embarrassed both him and his fellow emigrants. To give up one's original language required painful, if unconscious, repression. Self-justification and boasting that the new environment was better only partly helped to assuage the discomforts of abandoning one's earliest values. Perhaps the hardest identity to give up concerned food habits. As they became more successful economically, most immigrants emulated the eating style of the upper classes in Italy, not those of other Americans. Stores where they did their daily shopping were operated by and for Italians.

Discrimination against Italian immigrants persisted in all parts of the United States. In the South, outside the French Louisiana pocket of foreign influence, intolerance was at least as strong as in Northern urban centers. Foreigners were exploited, as were the blacks and other poor whites with whom they competed. Discrimination was somewhat less pronounced in the West. As we have seen, Italians who went into farming eventually purchased land and settled in rural areas. Their lives usually followed the pattern set by earlier settlers rather than replicated an old-world atmosphere. The fluidity of the West broke down past attitudes. Perhaps because of this, racial tension failed to develop in quite the same ways in *il Far Ouest.*

Fierce discrimination occurred in areas where large numbers of foreigners competed, as in the mining industry. Heavy surplus of unemployed immigrants led to strife. Friction between nationalities fueled local prejudice, especially when anti-Italian tensions exploded into riots as they did with Irish workmen. Particularly threatened by the influx of southern Europeans, the Irish popularized the terms "dago" and "wop," thereby contributing to the debasing stereotype which attached itself to the Italians. Americans unfairly looked upon the Italians as dark, lazy, dirty, and hysterically emotional—especially when angered.

The Italians themselves also confused their self-image. Centuries of division between North and South Italians affected discrimination against them. Northern Italy, historically, has evolved as part of central European culture, which was more industrialized and cosmopolitan. Conversely, southern Italy remained a deprived area toward which Northerners felt superior. Reacting to the Yankee scramble for economic advancement, some North Italians sought to emphasize whatever education or social status they had once possessed. Only by doing so could they cling to their individualism. But, in striving so hard for Americanization, the North Italians disparaged the status and achievements of Calabrians, Sicilians, Neapolitans and other Southerners.

In a kind of pecking order, the Piedmontese, Venetians, and Lombards, even in the New World, resented the fact that the swarthier, shorter Southerners represented the typical Italian in the minds of Americans. The Southerner's lack of education, his poverty, and his emotionalism repelled Northerners, who were considered reserved, tight, and unfeeling by Southerners.

Some North Italians, like racists of other nationalities, thought illiterate Southerners should have stayed in their peasant homeland. Once in the slums of America, they believed Southerners would turn to violence and crime. Numerous Northerners, however, were anarchists. For example, Bartolomeo Vanzetti, of the Sacco–Vanzetti case, was a Piedmontese. And labor disturbances tended to be instigated by North Italians.

Before Sacco and Vanzetti's time, labor agitation and foreigners had been linked in the public mind with organized crime. In 1890 an incident in New Orleans encouraged the notion that Italians were frequently associated with crime. A few Italians belonged to Southern groups that opposed anti-Negro discrimination, and this aroused animosity. White supremacy was, of course, prevalent, and since Italians were ignorant of the depth of racial feeling, they inadvertently encouraged mob violence. In New Orleans, after Italians began to run the fish and fruit trade, a series of crimes related to control of the waterfront suddenly occurred. People began to talk of "Mafia chieftains" and "Sicilian crimes." None of the alleged Mafia leaders were convicted of wrongdoing although the public suspected bribery of local officials. In March 1890, while he was investigating such charges, New Orleans Chief of Police David Hennessy was murdered. Although no one would identify the assassins, several Italians were arrested and nine suspects brought to trial. After six of them were acquitted and a mistrial declared for the other three, the press inflamed the populace, encouraging local citizens to attend a mass meeting to punish these "criminals." A vigilante mob broke into jail, seized 11 frightened Sicilians, including the nine who had already been tried, and hanged them. The police ultimately arrested more than 100 Italians during the antiforeignism that swept the city.

News of the New Orleans affair distressed all Italians. The Italian government demanded that the lynchers be punished and that an indemnity be paid. Secretary of State James G. Blaine replied that this was a matter of state jurisdiction, although President Benjamin Harrison publicly apologized. Italy withdrew her minister at Washington; then it was discovered that 8 of the 11 persons killed were naturalized citizens. The United States Congress voted $25,000 to be distributed among survivors of the three noncitizens. Italy then restored diplomatic relations.

The Louisiana lynchings also brought the criminal aspects of the Mafia to the attention of Americans. Exaggerated charges that the organization was behind much criminal activity were widely publicized. The term "Black Hand" originated in the United States. In western Sicily the Mafia was a regulatory group which originally developed out of disrespect for government by foreign rule, designed to punish criminals escaped from the law. Some of the "best" families became involved with the old Mafia. These persons were interested not only in land and money but in power as well. The term Mafia, so commonly used by non-*Mafiosi,* is never employed by the Sicilians most involved. Instead, they prefer to call themselves *"amici,"* or "friends." Sometimes they use the phrase, *"L'onorata società,"* or society of friends. A sacred duty, known as *"omertà,"* makes it dishonorable to turn to the authorities, especially the police, in order to right a wrong. To do so is to court punishment, even death, usually in the middle of the night by unknown assailants.

The American obsession with Mafia folklore includes a popular belief that a series of loosely organized criminal groups exist not only in western Sicily but also as a worldwide syndicate with branches in every American city. Joseph Albini's study of the American Mafia attempts to pinpoint the genesis of this legend. Based upon information gained from police and underground sources, he refutes the idea of a cohesive group we can label the "Mafia" or "Cosa Nostra." However, a number of American syndicates, some of them peopled and led by Italo–Americans, do engage in a variety of illegal enterprises, utilizing bribery, informers, infiltration techniques, as well as murder and torture.

Senator Estes Kefauver's committee investigation of organized crime in 1950–1951 (and a later one by the McClellan Committee in 1963) revealed no real evidence of the existence of a Mafia. A sense of mystery and intrigue, nevertheless, pervaded not only Kefauver's Senate investigation but all subsequent attempts to track down what the press luridly describes as a mysterious, unseen force that seeks to dominate the world. An almost paranoid fascination has settled upon historically confused attempts to trace the tentacles of this malignant octopus.

Insofar as there is an American Mafia, it appears to be held together by the kinship practices of the Sicilian past rather than as a monolithic national organization. Immigrant criminal activity tended to merge within relatively close families and neighborhoods as kin and townsfolk shared woes, successes, and status. Today's kinship codes, unspoken yet felt, are a holdover from an earlier period. Italo–Americans consider themselves libeled unfairly by naive persons who would like to believe that America's crime problem can be explained by blaming it on any one group, especially a foreign one.

In the United States, certain Sicilian kinship systems became massively corrupted by second-generation criminals from its city slums. If there is a "new Mafia" it represents diluted gangsterism. Both the Italian and American versions of such a phantom have no outward formal organization. They can be defined only as a loose familial coalition of men and groups, each working on a local level. Yet, this "brotherhood" may cooperate to control interests in the economic life of an area. Myths about the Mafia have seriously blackened the reputation of Italians in the United States even though, percentage-wise, the incidence of criminal conviction among Italian immigrants has actually been less than that among the native-born. Often the crimes that Italo–Americans committed were more dramatic and emotional than substantial. Newspapers headlined these as "crimes of passion," and only thoughtful writers blamed the overcrowding and close competition in metropolitan slums for such crime, seeing the big cities as havens for hoodlums turned gangsters.

The vast majority of Italian–Americans were, of course, law-abiding citizens who cringed from the stigma of criminality. As early as 1907, a White Hand Society was organized in Chicago to combat the notoriety of the Black Hand. This spread to other cities where Italians sought to alter their unfortunate image. Yet few persons even know that such a countervailing organization existed. The Mafia myth may satisfy the country's need for a scapegoat and foster the wish that sin has come from abroad. We do find it hard to believe that crime can be American—our own fault. And foreigners and other minorities have always been good whipping boys.

As a result, some Americans became uneasy about the passage of the Immigration Act of 1965, which liberalized existing immigration laws and eliminated the quota system. They feared further immigration from southern Europe and the crime they associated with it. It may be many years before the damaging reputation which the Italians so resent is altered.

Despite the Mafia, time and the success of Italians themselves have, however, helped to modify American bigotry toward them. During World War II, when the need for national unity was stressed, immigrants became more acceptable. During the early days of Mussolini, some of them had approved of his policies, but so had such Americans as Ezra Pound or Father Charles E. Coughlin. The Italo–American press had called attention to the dangers of Fascism long before public opinion here became aware of its dangers. During the 1930s a bevy of Italian intellectuals, journalists, and political exiles called *fuorusciti* had fled Italy. Among these anti-Fascists were Gaetano Salvemini, who began an American career as a professor and writer; Carlo Sforza, who was later Italian Foreign Minister; Giuseppe Borgese, author of the savage attack on Fascism entitled *Goliath;* Max Ascoli, founder of the liberal journal *The Reporter;* and Alberto Tarchiani, who fled to France and became Italy's first postwar ambassador to the United States. We have already mentioned atomic physicist Enrico Fermi's escape from Italy.

When World War II broke out, President Franklin Roosevelt leaned heavily upon the persuasive support of Generoso Pope on the East Coast and A. P. Giannini in the West, attempting to communicate governmental issues and aims to the Italian community. Any fears that might have existed concerning the loyalties of Italians were, however, groundless. In the New York area, Americans of Italian descent led any other national group in volunteer military enlistments. No Italian engaged in espionage or sabotage during the war. No Italo–American has ever been tried for treason.

By the 1960s, a move to fight the defamation of Italian–Americans culminated in the founding of an organization called "Americans of Italian Descent" which had 60,000 members by 1972. A series of protest demonstrations took place in New York City. To WASPs, these ethnic rallies seemed almost paranoid in self-pity. Paradoxically, although working-class persons with Italian names had once "wrapped themselves in the flag," some of them now lashed out at the FBI as well as at a hostile press which pictured them as Mafia-ridden. As government crackdowns on the Mafia continued, the Italian–Americans became deeply concerned over their personal respectability and image; they accused the news media of rank partisanship. The sensationalism of both television and newspapers, they said, was responsible for continued portrayal of Italians as violent and emotional.

At the 1972 premiere of *The Godfather* in Kansas City, local Italians bought up every seat but the film played to an empty theater.

As Italian–Americans became more secure of their position in America, they depended less on the institutions that had supported them as immigrants. Italo–American newspapers had always specialized in folksy advice, reported events in Italy, and detailed local news. Most such papers became weeklies; dailies survived only in large cities. After World War II, editors found it more difficult to fill their pages with material cribbed from homeland papers. As American-born children formed new households, they began to read American journals only. After their parents died, subscriptions to Italian-language papers were not renewed. Various immigrant newspapers folded because former readers no longer needed to look back to the old country for reassurance. By then they had "assimilated," a term which itself became unpopular among members of the second and third generation of Italians.

Second- and third-generation Italians also did not require the mutual aid societies set up to offer help. Immigrants had once banded together in groups loyal to a special region in Italy. Hundreds of individual societies broadened their functions from insurance and protection to social activities. Gradually, the numbers of these organizations decreased as they merged. State insurance laws forced others to disband or to reincorporate. As larger groups brought together *paesani* from all parts of Italy, their sense of provincialism decreased. Those who had joined mutual benefit organizations contributed small monthly dues to guarantee that members were looked after when sick, out of work, or when they required funeral services.

Members of the third generation needed the support of the immigrant societies even less than their second-generation parents, although they revealed an interest in preserving their heritage by congregating with persons of similar background. Thus, a variety of cultural societies and service groups exist in large cities throughout the United States. Nationally, these include the Garibaldina lodges and Unico. Unico sponsors scholarships for students, sends needy children to summer camps, and expresses its civic and social maturity in other tangible, American-style ways.

Ethnic groups have varied widely in their attitudes toward education and entry into the professions. For the immigrant, to be a professional man meant to be able to choose one's friends (and even a wife) from a wider circle. Professional life also meant financial and social emancipation from the drudgery of blue-collar jobs. Yet, less educated Italians, in contrast to the Germans, Irish, and Jews, sometimes were more rigid in accepting social advancement.

As compared to another ethnic group, the Jews, one can see Italian deficiencies more clearly. Whereas Jews have always encouraged intellectual attainment among the young, many Italian parents feared that education would estrange them from their offspring. The Italian peasant family background continued to be remote from an educated life style. Many immigrant homes were bereft even of a single book. A negative attitude toward learning and intellectualism helps us understand why more persons of Italian descent are not a part of America's academic scene.

The early education of Italian children often did not encourage high academic achievement. Several factors contributed. First there was the peasant custom of terminating formal education at about age 14—as soon as legally possible—so that children could begin earning wages. This tended to create schools that were vocationally, not academically, oriented. Second, the generally low scores on IQ tests administered to Italian children in the early 1900s reinforced this orientation, although the results were disputed. Such tests were taken at face value without correcting for cultural differences, which we now know seriously bias their results. Third, the difficulties of learning in a foreign-language context were not fully recognized; only in schools operated by Italian priests or nuns could children learn in their native tongue. Equally important, many immigrants who had not themselves been well educated were hostile to intellectual achievement by their children.

Some members of the first generation transformed English words into a common jargon useful among Italians who did not understand each other's regional dialects: for example, rag, bar, and car became *raggo, barro,* and *carro;* grocery was *grosseria;* icebox became *isabox.* This was an early step toward becoming Americanized, although some groups maintained their dialects as well. Other persons changed their names: Tomassini became Thomas; Lombard came from Lombardi. The novelist Lucas Longo, in his *Family on Vendetta Street,* gives us a glimpse of the agony of a father named Bentolinardo, who, after struggling to send his son through medical school, sees him put up a sign lettered "Dr. Bentley."

As time passed, intense differences caused continuing tension between first- and second-generation Italians. Children were often taught to mistrust those outside the family. But such strong family unity seemed without function in an open, more democratic environment in which the young no longer misinterpreted the competition of neighbors as a threat to their existence. Instead, the American ethos emphasized individual achievement in cooperation with others. As cultural inhibitions weakened, immigrant children became more independent, and they sought to cast off parental reliance upon foreign values. With material success came an erosion of that strict family closeness and authority of former times. No longer could the male patriarch remain the undisputed head of the family. No longer could a mother's meekness conceal a strong spirit that covertly equaled her husband's domineering will.

In the process, a reversal of generations occurred. It was ironic that children should teach their parents the concepts of American life and interpret the new society to them. This was the opposite of the European experience, in which the older generation continued firmly in command virtually until death.

Gradually, members of the second generation moved into better neighborhoods and sought prestige in other ways. This confused yet another traditional Italian concept. Keeping one's place in society's hierarchy was expected. To move up was an impertinence. Not all members of the first generation, of course, shunned social and economic standing. Nevertheless, parents often nursed regrets that they, themselves, had not had the opportunities or sense of freedom their children had. Foremost among these was education. In short, a few first-generation Italians resented the successes of their children. As Phyllis Williams explains:

Many misunderstandings spring up over such differences that promote the sense of fear, the feeling of insecurity, and the belief that prestige is declining. Herein lies the explanation of the defensive attitude which turns immigrants not only against the world outside their doors but sometimes even against those who have hitherto been most dear to them—their own children.[1]

---

[1] Phyllis H. Williams, *South Italian Folkways in Europe and America: A Handbook for Social Workers, Visiting Nurses, School Teachers,* rev. ed. (New York, 1969). This book was originally published in 1938.

The first generation, understandably, wished to display its success before relatives and friends in the old country. Returning immigrants invested their savings in diamonds, gold-filled teeth, or expensive clothes. Carrying bulging suitcases, these returnees became familiar figures in Italian villages. Some were persuaded to remain in Italy because they could afford a higher standard of living then ever before. They bought Fiat autos, two-story homes, and promptly forgot their broken English. In America they had been foreigners—dagos— but in their Italian village they were "the Americans."

Those who had become too Americanized were eager to return home with renewed sympathy for the United States. As for the second generation, few of them ever saw the *Italia* of their parents. Not until the Second World War did they, furthermore, show much interest in the homeland of their ancestors. While they may have admired it culturally or physically, it had become a faraway mythological construct, and some chose to deny its influence upon them. Others found in Italy not only antiquity, but unexpected modernity in autos, housing, and in the world of fashion.

Recent immigrants from Italy have felt less discrimination than formerly. They have frequently been better educated and more affluent. Current immigration laws encourage professional persons to apply for visas, and the quality of immigrants' education—rather than their origin or total number of immigrants—has become important. Under the Immigration and Nationality Act Amendments of 1965 (which came into force in 1968), the old national-origin quota arrangement was replaced by a system of preferences based upon family relationship to United States citizens, whether the immigrant's skills were needed, and whether political asylum was a factor. Whereas only about 5000 persons could enter from Italy under the Act of 1924, in 1969 immigration officials admitted 24,465 persons. That year Italy ranked first in the number of visas issued. And 24,481 more Italians were admitted during 1970. Close relatives of permanent residents are now accorded some preference for admission while skilled aliens whose services are urgently needed receive first preference.

No longer do most immigrants fall within the unskilled category of workers, unwanted and sometimes despised. Northern Europe, which had formerly supplied a high proportion of laborers, now provides fewer immigrants. What were once called the "old" and "new" immigration periods are both over. For older immigrants, the memory of the beloved homeland has faded. Although its beauty was cherished and idealized unconsciously, each had formed his own vision not only of the old country, but also of the new homeland. These impressions were reflected in the mark each individual made in the United States.

Chapter Twelve Bibliography

Adjustment to life in America by Italians is treated in Pisani, *The Italian in America;* Iorizzo and Mondello, *The Italian–Americans;* Rolle, *The Immigrant Upraised;* Tomasi and Engel, *The Italian Experience;* Irvin L. Child, *Italian or American? The Second Generation in Conflict* (New Haven, 1943); Leonard Covello, *The Social Background of the Italo–American School Child* (Leiden, 1967); and E. P. Hutchinson, *Immigrants and Their Children, 1850–1950* (New York, 1936). Consult also Salvatore John La Gumina, ed., "Ethnicity in American Political Life: The Italian American Experience," *Proceedings of the First Annual Conference of the American Italian Historical Association,* October 26, 1968; Antonio Mangano, *Sons of Italy, a Social and Religious Study of the Italians in America* (New York, 1917); and Enrico C. Sartorio, *Social and Religious Life of Italians in America* (Boston, 1918). A recent autobiography, Joseph N. Sorrentino, *Up from Never* (New York, 1971) tells of an Italian growing up in a Brooklyn ghetto.

The literature on Sacco and Vanzetti is extensive; a good starting point is Herbert B. Ehrmann, *The Case That Will Not Die: The Commonwealth of Massachusetts* vs. *Sacco and Vanzetti* (New York, 1970), as well as Francis Russell, *Tragedy in Dedham* (New York, 1962).

The Mafia is dealt with in Frederick Sondern, Jr., *Brotherhood of Evil: The Mafia* (New York, 1959); Joseph Albini, *The American Mafia, Genesis of a Legend* (New York, 1971); Luigi Barzini, Jr., *From Caesar to the Mafia* (London, 1971); and "The Real Mafia," *Harper's Magazine,* 208 (June 1954), 38–46. See also Puzo's *The Godfather* and Gay Talese, *Honor Thy Father* (New York, 1971), based on the life of Joseph Bonanno. Other volumes that touch this subject include Harry J. Anslinger and Will Oursler, *The Murderers* (New York, 1961); Daniel Bell, *The End of Ideology* (New York, 1962) and the popular but poorly documented Ed Reid, *Mafia* (New York, 1964). Apt to be overlooked is Giovanni Schiavo, *The Truth about the Mafia and Organized Crime in America* (New York, 1962).

Some recent books on crime and the Mafia are actually rewrites of an early volume by Fred Pasley entitled *Al Capone, the Biography of a Self-Made Man* (New York, 1931). A book written from the premise that there is a real and dangerous Mafia is Nicholas Gage, *The Mafia Is Not an Equal Opportunity Employer* (New York, 1971).

Epilogue

Attitudes toward minorities have undergone subtle and important changes. The Irish were perhaps the first nationality to respond to the prevailing American society by acculturation, the first to prove their respectability to the WASP establishment, eventually producing an American president. Gradually, other minorities changed their attitudes toward assimilation. Recently, blacks have maintained that "black is beautiful" and have used militant means to secure their rights. Following the example of the blacks, today Indians, Orientals, Poles, and Italians—minorities which once felt ashamed of their origins—have begun to proclaim ethnic pride. Even some white ethnics who insist they will not adapt to the American system are a bit late in the nation's demographic history. This new ethnicity seems due to the third generation's need to find out who they are, who their forebears were, and where they are from. It is a search for self-identity by persons who are part of a white minority of "Eurocrats" rather than part of some racial or ethnic tradition.

A search for the past extends to nonethnics as well. In America's largest cities it is the WASPs who are increasingly outnumbered as one city block after another is filled with Puerto Ricans, Chicanos, or Jews—all groups with distinctive roots. Some nonethnic Americans yearn for rediscovery of their personal history, too, as if to compensate for an indefinite past devoted largely to amassing wealth rather than to preserving a viable heritage.

In the 1920s, a novel about Studs Lonigan, the Portnoy of his time, did not strike the same responsive public chord that films and novels about immigrants do today. During that intolerant decade, two genuine foreign heroes, Sacco and Vanzetti, were kept behind bars. The immigrant's years of fulfillment were not yet at hand.

Discrimination against immigrants had its roots in economic and social factors as well as ignorance, but a psychological explanation also illuminates the origins of prejudice. Perhaps the injustices heaped upon Italians in earlier days were a projection of majority anxieties, given voice in an adolescent America by extremists and bigots. Just as we displace onto others our inner fears, cultural guilt can be passed on from generation to generation.

Suddenly it has become desirable for both the defending majority and restive minorities to recapture their origins rather than to want only Americanization. An American Jewish novelist has turned a love-hate relationship with his culture into financial profit, just as an Italo–American writer has partly heroized members of the Mafia. *Portnoy's Complaint* and *The Godfather* are the result.

Today's truculent grandchildren of immigrants, no longer prime targets of hostility, wear red, white, and green buttons calling for "Italian power." They insist upon voicing their heritage at public rallies and more often than on certain feast days. The descendants of Italian immigrants may seem more willing to acknowledge both good and bad in their forefathers; but the Italian–American Civil Rights League and the Americans of Italian Descent proclaim, in essence, that he who is non-Italian has no right to make such judgments.

Other touchy young ethnics repudiate the materialistic aspirations of their forebears—as do many young Americans. The third generation also deplores the divisive secondary role which the first and second generation was willing to assume educationally and socially. Such repudiation shows a lack of historical sensitivity for the adversities of immigrants who once lived in a bigoted context, which shamed them into denying their origins.

Yet, perhaps only in that America of an earlier period could immigrants be twice-born. To emigrate was to have a second chance. After the Jews and the Irish became virtual establishment figures, a sense of satisfaction also settled over many American Italians. The hopeful emigration from Italy, the dismal circumstances upon arrival, the desperate struggle to succeed, repudiation or soft-pedaling of one's origins, the second-generation flight to the suburbs, and, lately, the celebration of these origins by the third generation—all are part of the Italian immigrant story. Today, its ethnic subculture survives in spite of the paradoxes of segregation and assimilation. Those American Italians who no longer find it necessary to deny their origins are rediscovering their cultural history.

INDEX